基于潜变量模型的
测量不变性检验方法比较研究

Comparison of Methods for Detecting Violations of
Measurement Invariance Using Latent Variable Modeling

张明才 著

中国海洋大学出版社

·青岛·

图书在版编目（CIP）数据

基于潜变量模型的测量不变性检验方法比较研究：
英文 / 张明才著 . -- 青岛：中国海洋大学出版社，
2023.4

　　ISBN 978-7-5670-3460-0

　　Ⅰ. ①基… Ⅱ. ①张… Ⅲ. ①统计模型－研究－英文
Ⅳ. ① C81

中国国家版本馆 CIP 数据核字（2023）第 047049 号

出版发行	中国海洋大学出版社		
社　　址	青岛市香港东路 23 号	邮政编码	266071
出 版 人	刘文菁		
网　　址	http://pub.ouc.edu.cn		
订购电话	0532-82032573（传真）		
责任编辑	邵成军	电　　话	0532-85902533
印　　制	日照日报印务中心		
版　　次	2023 年 4 月第 1 版		
印　　次	2023 年 4 月第 1 次印刷		
成品尺寸	170 mm ×230 mm		
印　　张	7.5		
字　　数	132 千		
印　　数	1—1 000		
定　　价	50.00 元		

Abstract

This book is a study on the application of three statistical methods, namely the free baseline method, the Benjamini-Hochberg method and the alignment method to identify the noninvariant measurement parameters at the indicator level under the framework of latent variable modeling. On a comprehensive review of previous related studies, this book investigates the pros and cons of these three methods under both simulation and empirical conditions.

Measurement invariance refers to the fact that the measurement instrument measures the same concept in the same way in two or more groups. However, in educational and psychological testing practice, the assumption of measurement invariance is often violated due to the contamination by possible noninvariance in the measurement models. Under the framework of latent variable modeling, methodologists have developed different statistical methods to identify the noninvariant components. Among these methods, the free baseline method is popularly employed, but this method is limited due to the necessity of choosing a truly invariant reference indicator. Two other methods, namely, the Benjamini-Hochberg and the alignment method are exempt from the reference indicator setting. The Benjamini-Hochberg method applies the false discovery rate procedure. The alignment method aims to optimize the model estimates under the assumption of approximate invariance.

The purpose of the present study is to address the problem of reference indicator setting by comparing the Benjamini-Hochberg method and the alignment method with the traditional free baseline method through both a simulation study and an empirical data analysis. More specifically, the simulation study is designed to investigate the performances of the three methods through varying the sample sizes and the characteristics of noninvariance embedded in the measurement models. The characteristics of noninvariance are distinguished as the location of noninvariant parameters, the degree of noninvariant parameters, and the magnitude of model noninvariance. The performances of these three methods are also compared on an empirical dataset (Openness for Problem-Solving Scale in PISA 2012) that is obtained from three countries (China, Australia, and the United States).

The simulation study finds that the wrong reference indicator choice heavily impacts the free baseline method, which produces high Type I error rates and low statistical power rates. Both the Benjamini-Hochberg method and the alignment method perform better than the free baseline method in this setting. Comparatively speaking, the benefit of the Benjamini-Hochberg method is that it performs the best by achieving high powers for detecting noninvariance. The power rate increases with lowering the magnitude of model noninvariance, and with increasing sample size and degree of noninvariance. The alignment method performs the best with respect to Type I errors. The Type I error rates estimated by the alignment method are low under all simulation conditions. In the empirical study, both the Benjamini-Hochberg method and the alignment method perform similarly in estimating the invariance/ noninvariance patterns among the three country pairs. However, the free baseline method, for which the reference indicator is the first item by default, recovers a different invariance/noninvariance pattern. The suggestions on which method is better used for model noninvariance detection are discussed and elaborated.

The results can help the methodologists gain a better understanding of the potential advantages of the Benjamini-Hochberg method and the alignment method over the traditional free baseline method. The study results also highlight the importance of correctly specifying the model noninvariance at the indicator level. Based on the characteristics of the noninvariant components, practitioners may consider deleting/modifying the noninvariant indicators or free the noninvariant components while building partial invariant models in order to improve the quality of cross-group comparisons.

Key to Abbreviations

LVM	Latent Variable Modeling
MGCFA	Multi-Group Confirmatory Factor Analysis
MI	Measurement Invariance
DIF	Differential Item Functioning
RI	Reference Indicator
FDR	False Discovery Rate
FR	Free Baseline
B-H	Benjamini-Hochberg
AM	Alignment
PMI	Partial Measurement Invariance
CI	Confidence Interval
LRT	Likelihood Ratio Test
PISA	Programme for International Student Assessment
USA	United States of America
AUG	Australia
CHN	China
SEM	Structural Equation Modeling
MLCFA	Multilevel Confirmatory Factor Analysis
FWER	Family Wise Error Rate

Table of Contents

List of Tables

List of Figures

Chapter 1 ≫

An Overview

1.1 Introduction

In the field of educational and psychological measurement, the cross-group comparison of latent constructs is inevitably applied in many situations, for instance, in a comparative study of students' mathematics scores across different classes in the same city, state, country, or across different nations worldwide. Latent Variable Modeling (LVM) is one of the basic techniques to accomplish this goal under the assumption of Measurement Invariance (MI) (Millsap, 2011; Meredith, 1993; Dimitrov, 2010; Widaman & Reise, 1997; Steenkamp & Baumgartner, 1998; Schmitt & Kuljanin, 2008; Vandenberg & Lance, 2000). The basic idea of MI is that the measurement instrument measures the same concept in the same way in two or more groups to warrant subsequently the possibility of a meaningful group comparison (Meredith, 1993; Steenkamp & Baumgartner, 1998; Vandenberg & Lance, 2000; Millsap, 2011). In other words, once MI fulfills, the respondents from different groups that have the same position on a latent trait of interest should provide a similar response (Mellenbergh, 1989; Barendse et al., 2010; Meredith, 1993; Millsap & Yun-Tein, 2004).

However, in educational practice, the violation of MI may occur in cross-group comparisons. The technique of multi-group confirmatory factor analysis (MGCFA) has been widely used to study the violation of MI across groups (Jöreskog, 1971; Byrne et al., 1989; Little, 1997; Steenkamp & Baumgartner, 1998; Vandenberg & Lance, 2000). One representative approach in MGCFA to identify the noninvariant components in a measurement model is the free baseline (FR) method, which was first named by item response theory (IRT) methodologists to detect differential item functioning (DIF) during the analysis of categorical data (Flowers et al., 2002; Meade & Lautenschlager, 2004; Stark et al., 2006). With this traditional method, all indicator parameters are free to vary across groups except for one reference indicator (RI) whose loading is fixed to one (Flowers et al., 2002; Meade & Lautenschlager, 2004; Stark et al., 2006; Jung & Yoon, 2016; Cheung & Rensvold, 2002). Once the RI is selected, other model parameters can be estimated in reference to the metric underlying it (Bollen, 1989; Mead & Wright, 2012; Cheung & Rensvold, 2002). The FR method has been widely adopted by researchers as a means of studying measurement parameter noninvariance (Meade & Lautenschlager, 2004; Stark et al., 2006; Jung & Yoon, 2016; Vandenberg & Lance, 2000).

1.2 Statement of the Problem

Multiple problems have been pointed out by methodologists over the years in relation to this traditional testing method, which are mainly concerned with the use of RI (Raykov et al., 2012, 2019; Johnson et al., 2009; Lopez Rivas et al., 2009; Cheung & Rensvold, 1999; Yoon & Millsap, 2007; Little et al., 2006). In educational practice, the choice of RIs within the FR method can pose serious problems. To make the noninvariance testing feasible, the RIs have to be assumed group invariant. However, this apriori assumption is often problematic if the choice of RIs is not sufficiently supported by past studies, theory or substantive knowledge. The selection of an inappropriate RI may cause severe Type I/Type II errors associated with the tests of measurement parameters (Johnson et al., 2009; Cheung & Rensvold, 1999; Yoon & Millsap, 2007; Lopez Rivas et al., 2009; Raykov et al., 2012, 2019).

Researchers developed other statistical methods to circumvent these possible problems caused by RI selection in MGCFA (Raykov et al., 2013; Yoon & Millsap, 2007; Cheung & Rensvold, 1998; Cheung & Lau, 2012; Finch & French, 2008a, 2008b; Asparouhov & Muthén, 2014; Oberski, 2014). Two of the methods, namely, the Benjamini-Hochberg (B-H) method (Benjamini & Hochberg, 1995; Raykov et al., 2013) and the alignment (AM) method (Asparouhov & Muthén, 2014), were found to perform well in exploring noninvariance without having to fix an RI.

The B-H method is conducted starting with a fully-constrained baseline model and by controlling the false discovery rate (FDR; Benjamini & Hochberg, 1995; Raykov et al., 2013, 2018; Williams et al., 1999; Steinberg, 2001). That is, the application of the B-H method commences with the full invariance assumption with respect to all threshold and loading parameters associated with all indicators in a given modeling setting. The next step is to determine the noninvariant indicators by releasing one constrained parameter at a time. As this full parameter invariance assumption for the fully-constrained baseline model may be violated due to the contaminated noninvariant indicators (Yoon & Millsap, 2007; Kim & Yoon, 2011; Whittaker, 2012), a B-H rejection threshold is adopted to reduce the occurrence of falsely rejecting tested individual hypotheses while maintaining a high level of power (Benjamini & Hochberg, 1995; Raykov et al., 2013).

Unlike the FR method and the B-H method, the AM method does not depend on any equality imposition/relaxation of model parameters (Asparouhov & Muthén, 2014; Flake & McCoach, 2018; Jang et al., 2017). In other words, no RI choice is needed and no nested model comparison is conducted for noninvariance testing by using this method. Instead, the largest extent of approximation of MI (if not fully accomplished thereby) is achieved through the optimization of parameter estimates using a component loss function (Jennrich, 2006). Whether one indicator parameter is noninvariant or not is determined by a postestimation procedure after the optimization process is completed (Asparouhov & Muthén, 2014; Flake & McCoach, 2018; Jang et al., 2017; Lomazzi, 2018; Munck et al., 2018; Byrne & Vijver, 2017).

The effectiveness of the B-H method and the AM method has been evaluated by researchers using either simulation designs or empirical data (Raykov et al., 2013; Williams et al., 1999; Steinberg, 2001; Asparouhov & Muthén, 2014; Flake & McCoach, 2018; Jang et al., 2017; Lomazzi, 2018; Munck et al., 2018; Byrne & Vijver, 2017). For example, in the Williams et al.'s (1999) simulation study, the B-H method demonstrated higher powers than both simple and sequential Bonferroni adjustment in multiple comparisons. Steinberg (2001) applied the B-H method to evaluate DIF in the Anger Experience and Expression Scale. The results showed that this method was effective in identifying DIF items. To avoid the necessity of choosing an RI for testing parameter invariance, Raykov et al. (2013) outlined the B-H testing procedure and applied it to correctly identify the noninvariant model parameters using a simulation design. However, no comprehensive simulation studies have been conducted using this method to detect measurement noninvariance.

To evaluate the performance of the AM method, Flake & McCoach (2018) conducted a simulation study for MI testing of polytomous items under conditions of partial MI. They found that the AM method adequately recovered parameter estimates under small and moderate amounts of noninvariance and worked better for the thresholds than for the loadings. Using an empirical dataset from the Satisfaction With Life Scale (SWLS), Jang et al. (2017) compared the alignment optimization procedure with MGCFA and multilevel confirmatory factor analysis (MLCFA) to investigate the source of SWLS noninvariance. Results indicated that all three methods consistently reported the same set of noninvariant intercepts. Likewise, other recent empirical studies (Lomazzi, 2018; Munck et al., 2018; Byrne & Vijver, 2017) also confirmed that the AM method, as an alternative to MGCFA, is a valuable tool for evaluating measure/survey quality and comparability, discovering indicator noninvariance, and substantiating the trustworthiness of the latent construct comparison across groups.

Although the above-mentioned B-H method and the AM method have demonstrated their capability in detecting the violations of MI at indicator level, their performances are not compared either in simulation or empirical cross-group studies, especially how well they will perform as compared with the FR method. It is commonly acknowledged that the specification of noninvariance can be impacted by the sample size, the number of indicators, and characteristics of noninvariance, such as the location of noninvariant parameters, degree of noninvariance, and proportion of noninvariant indicators. However, we are unaware of the performances of these three methods under various noninvariance conditions that may occur in practical situations.

1.3   Purpose and Significance of the Study

The purpose of the present study is to address this concern by comparing the B-H method and the AM method with the FR method using both a simulation study and an empirical data analysis. The present research has both theoretical and practical implications. First, this study is to our knowledge the first to systematically compare two measurement noninvariance detection methods without fixing an RI with the traditional FR method, in which the pre-selected RI is inevitable. The results will help the methodologists gain a better understanding of the potential problems caused by mistakenly selected RI while applying the traditional FR method and the potential advantages of the B-H method and the AM method in this regard. Second, the study stresses the importance of correctly identifying the patterns of MI violations. This provides the practitioners with useful information on the characteristics of the noninvariant components in practical data structures. Based on these characteristics, they could consider delete/modify the noninvariant indicators or free these noninvariant components to pursue partial MI, and improve the validity of multiple-group comparisons.

1.4   Organization of the Book

This book consists of five chapters, each following a similar framework, starting with an introduction and ending with a summary. Chapter 1 is an overall introduction, which introduces the general background for the study of measurement noninvariane under the framework of latent variable modeling. Chapter 2 presents an overview of the theoretical background of the MI, and then provides background information for violations of MI and methods for detecting measurement noninvariance. This chapter also contains a general review of the literature on the detection methods of measurement noninvariance. Chapter 3 describes a simulation study which investigates the effectiveness of applying the three statistical methods, namely the FR method, the B-H method, and the AM method, to detect measurement noninvariance under different simulation conditions. Chapter 4 introduces the performances of the three statistical methods in an empirical dataset (Openness for Problem-Solving

Scale in PISA 2012) that is obtained from three countries (China, Australia, and the United States). Chapter 5 illustrates the implications and future recommendations of the current study. Recommendations on how to apply the three different statistical methods under different situations are discussed.

Chapter 2 ≫

Theoretical Background of Measurement Noninvariance

2.1 Introduction

This chapter first presents an overview for the concept of MI in LVM. It then proceeds with background information for the different levels of MI. Next, the violations of MI are discussed, and the last section elaborates on the three methods of noninvariance testing in previous studies.

2.2 The Concept of MI in LVM

The topic of MI has been highlighted in many cross-group comparison studies in LVM (Vandenberg & Lance, 2000). It is treated as a necessary condition for making valid inferences on similarities and differences of latent constructs in distinct populations (Millsap & Meredith, 2007; Raykov et al., 2012). As the latent constructs are manifested by multiple observed indicators in LVM, the measurement parameters of these proxy variables have to be assumed as group invariant to guarantee the comparability of the underlying constructs.

Mathematically, the assumption of MI for latent constructs requires the independence of conditional probability distributions of the observed scores. According to Mellenbergh (1989), the condition of MI is realized when

$$f(X \mid W, V) = f(X \mid W), \tag{1}$$

where X is a vector of observed variables (which are assumed to be multivariate normally distributed), W is a vector of latent variables underlying X, and V is an indicator for group membership.

Hence, for the MI assumption to be realized, observed scores X have to be conditionally independent given the underlying latent variable W, regardless of any grouping variable V. Specifically, MI requires that conditional on the latent factor scores, the expectation of observed scores, the covariances between the observed variables, and the unexplained variance unrelated with the latent factors should be all equal across groups. Hence, the MI requirement is a rather stringent condition and the conditional independence of observed scores can be easily violated.

Within the LVM framework, the commonly-used statistical method for checking MI is the MGCFA (Jöreskog, 1971; Vandenberg & Lance, 2000). In an MGCFA model, the latent variable is indirectly measured through one set of observed variables in each group. Each observed value is virtually decomposed as:

$$y_{ikg} = v_{kg} + \lambda_{kg}\eta_{ig} + \varepsilon_{ikg}, \tag{2}$$

where $i = 1, \ldots, N_g$ is the ith observation in group g; $k = 1, \ldots, K$ is the kth observed indicator; $g = 1, \ldots, G$ is the gth group. The distribution assumptions for the latent factor η_{ig} and the unique factor ε_{ikg} are $\eta_{ig} \sim N(\kappa_g, \phi_g)$ and $e_{ikg} \sim N(0, \theta_{kg})$.

In its vector format, the observed scores and its corresponding latent factors in group g are linearly related as:

$$\boldsymbol{Y}_g = \boldsymbol{v}_g + \boldsymbol{\Lambda}_g\boldsymbol{\eta}_g + \boldsymbol{\varepsilon}_g, \tag{3}$$

$$E(\boldsymbol{\eta}_g) = \boldsymbol{\kappa}_g, \tag{4}$$

$$Var(\boldsymbol{\eta}_g) = \boldsymbol{\Phi}_g, \tag{5}$$

$$Var(\boldsymbol{\varepsilon}_g) = \boldsymbol{\Theta}_g, \tag{6}$$

where $\boldsymbol{Y}_g$ represents a vector of observed scores on k measured variables, $\boldsymbol{\eta}_g$ represents a vector of q latent scores on q latent variables, $\boldsymbol{\Lambda}_g$ represents $k \times q$ matrix of factor loadings, $\boldsymbol{v}_g$ represents a $k \times 1$ vector of intercepts, and $\boldsymbol{\varepsilon}_g$ represents a $k \times 1$ vector of measurement residuals that have zero means and are uncorrelated with the latent factors. $\boldsymbol{\kappa}_g$ represents a vector of $q \times 1$ latent factor means in the gth group; $\boldsymbol{\Phi}_g$ represents a $q \times q$ covariance matrix among the latent variables; and $\boldsymbol{\Theta}_g$ is the $k \times k$ covariance matrix among the measurement residuals in the gth group.

Under the assumption of multivariate normal distribution represented by Y_g, the expected values for the observed variables are:

$$E(\boldsymbol{Y}_g) = \boldsymbol{\mu}_g = \boldsymbol{v}_g + \boldsymbol{\Lambda}_g\boldsymbol{\kappa}_g, \tag{7}$$

where μ_g represents a vector of $k \times 1$ expected means of the observed variables in the gth group.

The covariances of the observed variables are:

$$Cov(Y_g) = \Sigma_g = \Lambda_g \Phi_g \Lambda_g' + \Theta_g \qquad (8)$$

where Σ_g represents a $k \times k$ covariance matrix of the observed variables.

To meet the requirement of fully-realized MI, the measurement parameters (Λ_g, v_g, Θ_g) in the MGCFA models have to be invariant across groups. Otherwise, the full MI cannot be realized. In this case, the invariance assumptions for the noninvariant parameters in Λ_g, v_g, and Θ_g have to be released to pursue some compromised forms of MI (i.e. partial MI). Depending on the characteristics of the measurement noninvariance pattern, the equality constraints for those noninvariant parameters can be relaxed at either the scale level or the indicator level.

2.3 Levels of MI

When the equality assumptions of the whole set of model parameters (Λ_g, v_g, and Θ_g) in MGCFA are relaxed at the scale level, four distinct and hierarchically ordered levels of MI are available: configural invariance (Horn et al., 1983), metric invariance (Meredith, 1993; Horn & McArdle, 1992), scalar invariance (Meredith, 1993; Steenkamp & Baumgartner, 1998), and strict invariance(Mullen, 1995; Singh, 1995).

2.3.1 Configural Invariance

The lowest level of MI is the configural invariance, which does not require any constraints for the three types of measurement parameters (i.e. Λ_g, v_g, and Θ_g). The configural invariance only concerns with the invariance of model configuration across groups (Horn & McArdle, 1992; Buss & Royce, 1975; Suzuki & Rancer, 1994; Byrne et al., 1989; Meredith, 1993; Vandenberg & Lance, 2000). In other words, the central requirement of configural invariance is that the same pattern of zero and non-zero loadings in Λ_g matrix holds for all groups. In the meantime, the parameters estimated in Λ_g matrix are allowed to vary freely across groups. A tenable configural model implies that groups share one identical pattern of insignificant (zero) and significant (non-zero) factor loadings between observed variables and latent variables.

The utility of configural invariance model is limited as it does not involve the strict measurement scale consistency of the latent factors across groups. Its utility then mainly stems from the role as a baseline model, against which higher levels of MI with more restricted invariance requirements are evaluated.

2.3.2　Metric Invariance

In the MGCFA model, if we assume $\Lambda_g = \Lambda$ (the subscript g is dropped so that all factor loadings are group invariant), the resulting condition is denoted as metric invariance (Horn & McArdle, 1992), or weak MI (Meredith, 1993). Metric invariance requires only the plausibility of equal factor loadings across groups. It is a necessary condition for interpreting group differences in variances or covariances among latent variables.

2.3.3　Scalar Invariance

When both the measurement intercepts and factor loadings are assumed to be invariant ($\Lambda_g = \Lambda$, and $v_g = v$ for all k indicators), the resulting condition is denoted as scalar invariance (Steenkamp & Baumgartner, 1998), or strong MI (Meredith, 1993). Scalar invariance implies that group differences in the means of the observed variables are due to differences in the means of the underlying construct(s). When the imposed constraints in Λ and v matrices are statistically plausible, the retrieved scalar model provides substantively meaningful interpretations of cross-group differences in latent factor means and variances.

2.3.4　Strict Invariance

Beyond the requirement of equal factor loadings and equal intercepts in the scalar invariance model, the strict invariance requests an extra assumption of equal measurement residual variances contained in Θ_g matrix (that is, $\Theta_g = \Theta$). The cross-group invariance requirement for all the measurement parameters ($\Lambda_g = \Lambda$, $v_g = v$, and $\Theta_g = \Theta$) makes this model the most parsimonious one. When strict invariance holds, the observed variables in each group are measured with the same precision. All group differences from the observed variables are captured by and attributable to group differences on the common latent factors (Widaman & Reise, 1997).

2.4   Violations of MI

The MI tests described thus far are omnibus tests of whether the scale level invariance is fully satisfied or not. This is the common practice in empirical studies for the evaluation of measurement equivalence under the confirmatory factor analysis (CFA) framework (c.f. Vandenberg & Lance, 2000; Schimitt & Kuljanin, 2008; Steenkamp & Baumgartner, 1998; Putnick & Bornstein, 2016). As reviewed by Schimitt & Kuljanin (2008) and Putnick & Bornstein (2016), the majority of published empirical studies tested the metric invariance or scalar invariance. These articles covered a wide variety of areas in social and behavioral sciences (such as intelligence tests, life/job satisfaction, academic motivations). In these studies, the scale level invariance was demonstrated to support the applicability of the instruments across demographically diverse subgroups (such as gender, race, culture).

The popularity of scale level tests reflected a practical view toward the primary purpose of CFA-based MI testing. People hoped to verify the invariance at the scale level to warrant the subsequent cross-group comparisons (Davidov et al., 2014). However, in empirical situations, it is quite common that the measurement instruments are contaminated by noninvariant indicators. In such cases, the full invariance is not realized, particularly for those stringent forms beyond the configural invariance. The failure to establish MI poses great threat to the validity of cross-group comparison results (Davidov et al., 2014). For instance, if metric invariance is violated, the validity of cross-group comparison in terms of the latent factor variance would be in doubt. If scalar invariance does not hold, the validity of cross-group comparison in terms of latent means would be in question.

Recently, researchers started to notice that only performing scale level MI testing was not enough. This is because the scale level testing may miss sizable MI violations embedded in measurement models (e.g. Raykov et al., 2019). First, the plausibility of one scale level invariance does not mean that all the measurement parameters are truly invariant. It is possible that the noninvariance against one group could cancel out the noninvariance against another group within one model (Nye et al., 2019). Second, the criteria to judge whether one level of MI holds or not are commonly based on the significance of χ^2 change ($\Delta\chi^2$) (Byrne et al., 1989; Marsh & Hocevar, 1985; Reise et al., 1993). However, it is well known that the $\Delta\chi^2$ test is sample sensitive. The analysis at scale level may not have enough power to justify the critical deviations in case of small samples.

The indicator level nonequivalence testing has been frequently recommended to diagnose the source of any nonequivalence (Vandenberg & Lance, 2000). Research has shown that testing the parameters for a single indicator at a time provides a more accurate indication of noninvariance (Stark et al., 2006; Jung & Yoon, 2016; Raykov et al., 2013, 2019).

The accurate configuration of noninvariance pattern embedded in the dataset can benefit empirical data analysis in many ways. For example, those contaminated indicators whose parameters are largely different across groups can be simply ignored during the analysis. However, this option is usually not recommended because it is atheoretical and detrimental to the validity argument (Cheung & Rensvold, 1999). Another commonly used strategy is to use partial MI (PMI; i.e. partial scalar/metric invariance; Byrne et al., 1989). In these PMI models, the equality assumptions of these noninvariant components in Λ and v are released. Some researchers believed that two indicators with equal loadings and/or intercepts were sufficient for PMI (Byrne, et al., 1989; Steenkamp & Baumgartner, 1998). In more recent studies, researchers started to view the characteristics of noninvariance as a useful source of information to investigate why the cross-group invariance is absent (Davidov et al., 2012).

No matter which solution is adopted, researchers have to precisely identify those noninvariant indicators at first. Under the framework of LVM, three approaches show the promises for this purpose (Stark et al., 2006; Raykov et al., 2013; Asparouhov & Muthén, 2014): (1) the traditional FR method; (2) the B-H method, and (3) the AM method.

2.5 Methods of Detecting Measurement Noninvariance

2.5.1 The FR Method

The FR method is a relatively straightforward strategy to test the equivalence of loadings and intercepts across groups (Stark et al., 2006). One salient feature of this method is that the baseline model allows all indicator parameters free to vary except for one indicator which is chosen as RI for setting the common latent scale across groups. The invariance of individual indicator parameter is tested by comparing the baseline model with a nested model in which the tested parameter is constrained (Flowers et al., 2002; Meade & Lautenschlager, 2004; Stark et al., 2006; Jung & Yoon, 2016).

The CFA-based FR method was first adopted by IRT methodologists to compare its ability to detect DIF with the IRT-based methods (Flowers et al., 2002; Meade & Lautenschlager, 2004; Stark et al., 2006). They noticed that the performance of the FR method was comparable or better than other methods in some situations.

Flowers et al. (2002) proposed two MGCFA-based FR procedures, which were named as (i) slope procedure, and (ii) slope and intercept procedure, and compared these two procedures with non-linear IRT-based DIF method (NC-DIF procedure). The performances of these three procedures in detecting DIF were evaluated through a simulated test having 20 polytomous items. The results showed that the slope procedure successfully identified items that had differences in item discrimination parameters, but did not identify items different in threshold parameters. The slope and intercept procedure, and the NC-DIF procedure achieved contrary results as opposed to that by the slope procedure.

Stark et al. (2006) unified the CFA- and IRT-based methods and proposed a common DIF detection strategy, which was named as the FR method with Bonferroni correction. They compared the performance of this method with the constrained baseline method and the IRT-based method in a simulation study. They found that the three procedures performed similarly well in the majority of simulation conditions. The constrained baseline approach worked well only when no DIF items were present, and it exhibited a high Type I error rate when DIF was simulated on item thresholds. The FR method was found to perform well in all conditions.

In these previous studies, the simulated data were created to have a non-linear IRT measurement scale in order to allow for the comparison of the CFA- and IRT-based FR methods. The application of FR method was limited to the analysis of categorical data.

Jung & Yoon (2016) conducted a study, in which the simulated data were created based on partial invariance of continuous observed variables. In their study, the FR method was modified by using confidence interval (CI) to judge the invariance of parameters and named as forward CI method. They compared the performance of this method with two other commonly used methods, namely backward MI method (sequential use of the modification index) and the factor-ratio test under various simulated PMI conditions. They found that the forward CI method with 99% CIs has the highest perfect recovery rates and the lowest Type I error rates. The backward MI method performed similarly well with the more conservative criterion (MI = 6.635). Among all, factor-ratio test delivered the poorest performance, regardless of the chosen CI.

Nonetheless, the justification of the FR method in detecting indicator noninvariance has been questioned by many researchers (Jung & Yoon, 2016; Raykov et al., 2012, 2019; Cheung & Rensvold, 1999; Yoon & Millsap, 2007; Johnson et al., 2009; Lopez Rivas et al., 2009). The major concern with this method was that the RIs may not be truly invariant as they are supposed to be. The good performance of the FR method in the previous studies relied on the fact that one truly invariant indicator was selected as the RI. As admitted in the study by Yoon & Millsap (2007), the invariant indicator was known as a priori during simulation and was intentionally chosen for RI on purpose. However, invariant indicators are unknown in real data. To determine which indicators is truly invariant and can serve as the RI, it is not sufficient to only rely on the statistical evidence (Raykov et al., 2012).

To investigate the role of RIs in MI tests, Johnson et al. (2009) conducted a simulation study which examined the effects of RI selection at both scale and indicator level. The magnitude of RI difference was manipulated from 0.00 to 0.40 in 0.05 increments. The results indicated that an inappropriate RI selection had little effect on metric invariance, but poor RI choice produced very misleading results for indicator level tests. Consequently, group comparisons for MI were highly susceptible due to the poor RI choice.

2.5.2　The B-H Method

The original B-H method was proposed by Benjamini & Hochberg (1995) to address the low power rate of multiple hypothesis tests through an FDR controlling procedure. This procedure is instrumentally concerned with controlling the FDR, and thereby offers a way of increasing statistical power while maintaining an acceptable Type I error rate (Benjamini & Yakutieli, 2001).

After proposing their FDR controlling procedure, Benjamini & Hochberg (1995) conducted a simulation study to compare the power of this new method with two Bonferroni-type family wise error rate (FWER) controlling procedures (Bonferroni and Hochberg's procedure). They found that the benefits of using FDR controlling procedure are: (1) the power is uniformly higher than FWER controlling methods; (2) the power increases with the increase of the number of incorrect null hypothesis (i.e. the existence of true parameter difference in multiple testing); (3) the power increases with the increase of the total number of tested hypotheses.

Using empirical data from the NAEP Trial State Assessment (NAEP TSA), Williams et al. (1999) conducted a similar study to compare the performances of B-H FDR controlling procedure, Bonferroni procedure, and Hochberg's procedure in detecting measurement noninvariance. The results demonstrated that the B-H FDR controlling procedure obtained more reliable results than the other two procedures. This result was confirmed by the outcome of their following simulation studies. The B-H FDR controlling procedure was advantageous over the other two procedures especially when many comparisons were involved because its power remained stable as the number of comparisons increased.

In Steinberg's (2001) study, the potential DIF problems in developing the Anger Experience and Expression Scale were investigated. The IRT Likelihood Ratio Test (LRT) method was used to detect DIF and the significance level was adjusted using the B-H method. In her study, ten anger experience items and two anger expression items were found to be significantly different due to the context effect. This study showed the usefulness of B-H FDR controlling procedure to investigate DIF when a large number of hypotheses were tested.

In order to address the potential problems caused by the RI choice, Raykov et al. (2013) applied the B-H method for detecting indicator parameter noninvariance. The B-H method in MI testing was outlined there as a multi-step procedure based on the

B-H FDR controlling procedure and multiple individual restriction tests. Unlike the FR method, this method starts with a fully-constrained invariance model where all indicator parameters are constrained to be equal across groups. This fully-constrained baseline model is identified by defining the factor variance to one and the factor mean to zero in one selected group. The performance of this method was investigated in a simulation study in which one sizable noninvariant intercept was embedded in the simulated model. The results showed that the B-H method detected this noninvariant parameter with higher power than the conventional multiple testing procedures (Raykov et al., 2013). The application of B-H method limits the number of incorrect rejections of individual parameter constraints, and is preferred as a powerful tool to detect model noninvariance.

2.5.3 The AM Method

The AM method was initially developed with the goal to deal with MI testing when there are a large number of groups (Asparouhov & Muthén, 2014). It represents an alternative to the MGCFA technique for indicator level invariance testing (Muthén & Asparouhov, 2018; Flake & McCoach, 2018; Jang et al., 2017). Unlike the FR method and the B-H method, the AM method does not depend on any specified equality restrictions for both the loadings and indicator intercepts across groups (Asparouhov & Muthén, 2014; Flake & McCoach, 2018; Byrne & Vijver, 2017). Specifically, there is no need to choose a baseline model and sequentially add or release a particular constraint for invariance testing as in the MGCFA procedures. Instead, the AM method starts with a common configural model and then optimizes the estimates of the loadings and intercepts across groups to establish the most optimal MI pattern (Asparouhov & Muthén, 2014; Byrne & Vijver, 2017). The optimization process is realized by incorporating a loss function similar to the rotation criteria used in exploratory factor analysis (EFA; Asparouhov & Muthén, 2014).

After proposing the AM method, Asparouhov & Muthén (2014) conducted a series of simulation studies to evaluate the quality of this method. It was evaluated through analyzing a multiple-group data of 26 countries from the European Social Survey. These studies showed that this new method was a valuable alternative to the currently used MGCFA methods for studying MI. As the AM method was able to provide a detailed account of parameter invariance/noninvariance for every model parameter across groups, Asparouhov & Muthén (2014) argued that their proposed AM method can be used to test invariance of individual parameters.

Using a simulation design, Flake & McCoach (2018) extended the AM method to test MI in case of polytomous items. The various simulation conditions include the number of groups, proportion of noninvariant item parameters, magnitude of noninvariance, and type of noninvariance. They found that overall the method performed excellently in recovering the true parameters, and produced estimates with little bias, especially when the levels of noninvariance are small and medium. It also worked better for the thresholds than for the loadings.

To identify the noninvariant indicators for the Satisfaction With Life Scale (SWLS), Jang et al. (2017) analyzed an empirical data from 26 countries using three MI testing techniques: the AM method, MGCFA, and multilevel confirmatory factor analysis (MLCFA). The results indicated that all three methods consistently detected three noninvariant intercepts. The AM method has the advantage of providing indicator level and group-level MI information beyond general model information.

Byrne & Vijver (2017) compared the MGCFA and AM method in testing MI across 27 countries using an empirical dataset from the Family Values Scale designed to measure family functioning. They found that a large number of misspecified parameters (108 items) were identified when using the MGCFA method. However, the AM method revealed that only a small percentage of factor loadings (1.85%) and intercepts (17.2%) were noninvariant. Similarly, Lomazzi (2018) compared the AM method with MGCFA to assess the MI of gender role attitude scale in the World Values Survey. The results indicated that these two procedures converged in detecting the same item as the least invariant, and therefore,the alignment procedure is a valuable tool to assess MI as well as to detect noninvariant items.

Munck et al. (2018) applied the AM method to assess the MI for a pooled dataset from 46 countries. They found that the AM method is a valuable technique for identifying item noninvariance in surveys, and refining the administered instruments for the ultimate group comparisons.

Previous studies have found that the AM method can be applied to test invariance/noninvariance of parameters in factor analysis models(e.g. Byrne & Vijver, 2017; Jang et al., 2017). It should be noted that the fundamental assumption of the AM method is that there is a pattern of approximate MI in the data (Asparouhov & Muthén, 2014). More specifically, when the number of noninvariant parameters, as well as the extent of measurement noninvariance across groups is controlled at a minimum, the optimization of the AM method achieves the best effect. However, if this assumption is violated, the simplest and most invariant model achieved by the AM method might not be the true model. Muthén & Asparouhov (2014) recommended a rough rule of thumb for the application of this method: a limit of 25% noninvariance is safe for trustworthy alignment results. However, to what extent the performance of the AM method will be impacted by the violation of its fundamental assumption is not clearly demonstrated.

2.6　Chapter Summary

Based on the review of the previous literature, we can observe that the three above mentioned methods use different strategies to investigate the pattern of measurement noninvariance. The FR method applies the bottom-up strategy, in which the least number of equality restrictions is required in the baseline model. However, this method is limited by the potential danger of a wrong RI choice. In contrast, both the B-H method and the AM method avoid the problem of RI choice and address the concern of noninvariance detection through either controlling the FDR or minimizing a component loss function.

The study of measurement noninvariance is a complex problem which may be impacted by various factors. Among these factors, the sample size, the number of indicators, and the features of noninvariance embedded in the dataset are crucial ones studied in the literature.

Researchers noted that the commonly-used χ^2 difference ($\Delta\chi^2$) test is very sensitive to sample size (Brannick, 1995; Kelloway, 1995). As the sample size increases, $\Delta\chi^2$ will increase in power to reject the null hypothesis. The effectiveness of the FR method and the AM method in detecting measurement noninvariance is believed to be impacted by sample size (Stark et al., 2006; Jung & Yoon, 2016; Asparouhov & Muthén, 2014). The effect of sample size on the detection power of the B-H method is still not clearly known. In addition, the performance of the χ^2 statistics also varies by the number of indicators used to measure the latent traits (Herzog et al., 2007; Moshagen, 2012; Shi et al., 2018). According to the results of Shi et al. (2018), as the number of indicators increases, the empirical Type I error rates of the χ^2 statistics are inflated dramatically. Currently it is unclear to what extent the performance of the three above mentioned methods will be impacted by varying the number of indicators.

Research has also found that the features of noninvariance embedded in the data under investigation may impact the performance of different detection methods. The salient features of noninvariance include but are not limited to: 1) the location of noninvariant parameters (i.e. intercept, loading), 2) the noninvariance degree of noninvariant intercepts or loadings, and 3) the magnitude of model noninvariance. In this research, the magnitude of model noninvariance represents the percentage of noninvariant parameters within one measurement model. For example, if the percentage of noninvariant parameters is large, the probability of mistakenly choosing a wrong RI by the FR method may increase (Yoon & Millsap, 2007). For the B-H method, if numerous measurement parameters are noninvariant, the fully-constrained baseline models during the multiple individual restriction tests are more likely to be misspecified and the FDR may arise (Stark et al., 2006; Kim & Yoon, 2011; Whittaker, 2012). For the AM method, when the level of noninvariance contamination is high, the alignment results may not be trustworthy enough (Asparouhov & Muthén, 2014).

To date, no study has been conducted to compare the pros and cons of the three aforementioned methods for detecting measurement noninvariant components. Therefore, we are unaware about the performances of these three methods under various noninvariance conditions. Thus the purpose of the present study is to address this concern by comparing the B-H method, the AM method with the traditional FR method through both a simulation study and an empirical data analysis. More specifically, the study is designed to investigate the performances of the three methods through varying the sample sizes and the characteristics of noninvariance embedded in the measurement models. The characteristics of noninvariance are distinguished as the location of noninvariant parameters, the degree of noninvariant parameters, and the magnitude of noninvariance. The performances of these three methods are also compared through analyzing an empirical dataset (the index of Openness to Problem-Solving) that is obtained from three countries (China, Australia, and the United States) in PISA 2012. The study results will help educational practitioners to carry out a more informed choice of an indicator noninvariance detection method and improve the validity of multiple-group comparisons conducted in the empirical behavioral and social disciplines.

Chapter 3 ≫

Detection of Measurement
Noninvariance in a Simulated Study

3.1   Introduction

This chapter first introduces the simulation design of the study. A Monte Carlo simulation study is designed to investigate the performances of the FR method, the B-H method and the AM method in detecting measurement models with the violation of MI. Then the models for generating the data are described, followed by the interpretation of the data analysis procedures and evaluation criteria. Finally, the results of simulation study are reported.

3.2   Simulation Design

The simulation design includes both fixed conditions and manipulated conditions. For the fixed conditions, as shown in Table 3.1, two groups of respondents are assumed to be measured by continuous indicators, which are loaded on a single latent trait. One group is chosen as the reference group and the other as the focal group. These two groups are assumed to have an equal number of observations and the effect of unbalanced sample size is not considered.

Table 3.1   Fixed conditions in the simulation design

Fixed factors	Conditions
Number of groups	2
Number of latent factors	1
Loading parameter (λ)	0.5

(to be continued)

Fixed factors	Conditions
Intercept parameter (v)	0
Distribution of residual (ε)	$N(0, 0.75)$
Distribution of latent factor in the reference group (η_{ref})	$N(0,1)$
Distribution of latent factor in the focal group (η_{foc})	$N(0.5,1)$

In this simulation design, the loadings and intercepts of all indicators in both groups are initially set to be identical respectively. The loading parameters are standardized for the purpose to choose a representative value based on previous empirical studies. As reviewed by DiStefano (2002), the standardized loading parameters vary between 0.3 and 0.7 in majority of previous empirical CFA studies. Hence, the initial loadings are fixed at $\lambda = 0.5$ to represent an average standardized value. Meanwhile, the intercepts are fixed at $v = 0$. The residual variances are generated to create indicators with unit variance so that the residual variances are fixed at 0.75.

The residuals of all indicators are created to be normally distributed and uncorrelated with each other and the latent construct. The latent construct in the reference group is assumed to be distributed as standard normal (i.e. zero mean and unit variance). In the focal group, the latent construct is also assumed to be normally distributed with unit variance, but the latent mean is fixed at 0.5. The latent constructs in both groups are manifested by the same number of indicators.

In this simulation design, four conditions are manipulated, as summarized in Table 3.2. The manipulated factors include 1) sample size, 2) the location of noninvariant parameters, 3) the degree of parameter noninvariance, and 4) the magnitude of model noninvariance.

Table 3.2　Manipulated conditions in the simulation design

Manipulated factors	Conditions
Sample size (N)	200, 500, 1000
Location of noninvariant parameters	loading, intercept

(to be continued)

Manipulated factors	Conditions
Degree of parameter noninvariance (D)	
Loading (λ^D)	0.05 to 0.45 in 0.1 increments
Intercept (v^D)	0.10 to 0.90 in 0.2 increments
Magnitude of model noninvariance	
Proportion of noninvariant indicators	1/5, 2/5
Variation of noninvariance at the same indicator	partially, fully
Variation of indicator numbers (P)	3, 5, 7, 10

Sample size: Three sample sizes are selected (N = 200, 500, 1000 per group), representing small, medium and large sample size respectively. These sample sizes are selected by referring to previous research in studying sample size effect on measurement noninvariance detection (e.g. Stark et al., 2006; Mead & Lautenschlager, 2004; Muthén & Asparouhov, 2012).

Location of noninvariant parameters: Two types of measurement parameters are studied. Within one measurement model, the source of noninvariance is located at either loadings or intercepts.

Degree of parameter noninvariance: The degree of parameter noninvariance represents to what extent one noninvariant loading or intercept deviates from the MI requirement. In this study, the noninvariance degrees are built into the loadings or the intercepts separately. The values of modified intercepts/loadings in the focal group are modified to be higher than those fixed values in the reference group. The choice of simulated noninvariance degrees is based on the findings reported by Nye et al. (2019). As they reviewed in literature, the majority of standardized loading differences are below 0.10 and few are greater than 0.50; the majority of intercept differences are below 0.20, and few are above 1. Hence, to represent from minor to severe violations of MI, five noninvariance degrees are selected to modify the parameter noninvariance. The noninvariance degrees in loadings are selected from 0.05 to 0.45 in 0.1 increments (i.e. λ^D = 0.05, 0.15, 0.25, 0.35 or 0.45). The noninvariance degrees in intercepts are selected from 0.10 to 0.90 in 0.2 increments (i.e. v^D = 0.10, 0.30, 0.50, 0.70 or 0.90). The smallest values (λ^D = 0.05 and v^D =

0.10) represents negligible loading and intercept differences reported in nearly 60% of the previous studies (c.f. Nye et al., 2019).

Magnitude of model noninvariance: The magnitude of noninvariance in this study is defined as the percentage of noninvariant parameters within one measurement model. In general, the magnitude of noninvariance can be simulated in three different ways.

The first and also the most popular approach is to manipulate the proportions of noninvariant indicators (French & Finch, 2008; Meade & Wright, 2012).That is, to vary the number of noninvariant indicators with the total indicator number being fixed. To realize this simulation condition in this study, the total indicator number is fixed at five, which is the commonly applied scale length designed for Likert Scale questionnaires. Two proportions are then simulated: the low proportion (LP) and the high proportion (HP). In the LP condition, the first indicator (i.e. y_1) is modified to be noninvariant so that LP $= 1/5$. In the HP condition, the first two indicators (i.e. y_1 and y_2) are noninvariant so that HP $= 2/5$. Hence, the LP and HP conditions represent that 20% and 40% of the indicators are truly noninvariant within one model. This range of proportions is generally observed in empirical studies (e.g. Reise et al., 1993; Cheung & Rensvold, 1998). The noninvariance over 50% is rarely reported in empirical studies. This is because researchers usually believe that if the majority of indicators are noninvariant, the measured constructs in all groups will be hardly identical and comparable (Steenkamp & Baumgartner, 1998; Vandenberg & Lance, 2000).

Second, the magnitude of model noninvariance is represented by the number of noninvariant parameters located at the same indicator. To simulate this condition, only one of the five indicators (i.e. the indicator y_1) is modified to be noninvariant. In less contaminated models, this indicator is noninvariant at either the intercept or loading, which is addressed as a partially noninvariant indicator. In more contaminated models, this indicator is noninvariant at both the intercept and loading, which is addressed as a fully noninvariant indicator.

Third, the magnitude of model noninvariance can also vary with the change of indicator numbers loaded on the latent construct. To simulate this condition, the latent construct is measured by four different numbers of indicators ($P = 3$,

5, 7, or 10). This range of indicator numbers covers the commonly designed scale length to measure one construct in psychological and educational surveys (e.g. Moshagen, 2012; Yuan et al., 2015). When fixing one indicator (i.e. the indicator y_1) to be noninvariant, the models with few indicators are highly contaminated in the magnitude. In contrast, the models with a large number of indicators are less contaminated.

In sum, the present study's simulation conditions are composed of three sample sizes, two types of noninvariant parameter locations, five degrees of parameter noninvariance, and three ways to manipulate the magnitude of model noninvariance. Beyond the simulation conditions with embedded noninvariance in the models, one baseline condition in which all measurement parameters (i.e. all the intercepts and loadings) are set to be equal across groups is treated as the baseline data check.

3.3 Data Generation

The raw data for the two groups of subjects are generated using *Mplus* software (*Mplus* 7.4). In the reference group, the data for each indicator is generated based on the following model:

$$y_{i,k,ref} = 0.5\eta_{i,ref} + \varepsilon_{i,k,ref} \tag{9}$$

In this model, *ref* represents the reference group; i represents the ith observation; k represents the kth indicator. $y_{i,k,ref}$ represents the observed value of the ith observation on the kth indicator in the reference group; $\eta_{i,ref}$ represents the latent value of the ith observation in the referenced group and $\eta_{i,ref} \sim N(0,1)$; $\varepsilon_{i,k,ref}$ represents the residual for the ith observation on the kth indicator in the referenced group and $\varepsilon_{i,k,ref} \sim N(0, 0.75)$. Every $\varepsilon_{i,k,ref}$ is generated to be independently distributed across the indicators and also uncorrelated with $\eta_{i,ref}$. The intercept of the simulated indicator is zero. The standardized loading of the simulated indicator is 0.5. Since the latent variance is one and the residual invariance is 0.75, the indicator is generated to have a communality of 0.25 (c.f. Yoon & Millsap, 2007).

In the focal group, some indicators are generated to be invariant between two groups and the others are noninvariant. The response data for the between-group invariant indicators are generated following the model below.

$$y_{i,k,foc} = 0.5\eta_{i,foc} + \varepsilon_{i,k,foc}, \tag{10}$$

where *foc* represents the focal group, $\eta_{i,foc} \sim N(0.5,1)$, and $\varepsilon_{i,k,foc} \sim N(0, 0.75)$. Other terms have been defined previously. Every $\varepsilon_{i,k,foc}$ is generated to be independently distributed and uncorrelated with $\eta_{i,foc}$. Every indicator is generated to have a communality of 0.25.

In the focal group, the data for the manipulated noninvariant indicators are generated based on models different from Equation (10). Because the noninvariance can occur at either loadings, intercepts or both parameters, three different models are applied though adjusting the corresponding parameter values in Equation (10).

To generate data for those indicators with noninvariant loadings, Equation (10) is changed as:

$$y_{i,k,foc} = (0.5 + \lambda^D)\eta_{i,foc} + \varepsilon_{i,k,foc}, \tag{11}$$

where λ^D represents the noninvariance degree of the loading parameter (the subscript k for this term is dropped because within one model all the modified loadings are noninvariant at the same degree). Difference from Equation (10), the variance of $\varepsilon_{i,k,foc}$ is adjusted to allow the indicator to have unit variance. Hence, the adjusted variance of $\varepsilon_{i,k,foc}$ is $1 - (0.5 + \lambda^D)^2$. Correspondingly, every indicatoris generated to have a communality of $(0.5 + \lambda^D)^2$.

In the focal group, for those indicators with noninvariant intercepts, Equation (10) is changed as:

$$y_{i,k,foc} = v^D + 0.5\eta_{i,foc} + \varepsilon_{i,k,foc}, \tag{12}$$

where v^D represents the noninvariance degree of the intercept (the subscript k for this term is dropped because within one model all the modified intercepts are noninvariant at the same degree). Other terms have been defined before.

In the focal group, if one indicator is modified on both its loading and intercept, Equation (10) is changed as:

$$y_{i,k,foc} = v^D + (0.5 + \lambda^D)\eta_{i,foc} + \varepsilon_{i,k,foc}. \tag{13}$$

Similarly to the Equation (11), the variance of $\varepsilon_{i,k,foc}$ is adjusted to allow the indicator to have unit variance. Then, the adjusted variance of $\varepsilon_{i,k,foc}$ is $1 - (0.5 + \lambda^D)^2$. The communality of every $y_{j,k,foc}$ is $(0.5 + \lambda^D)^2$.

Each simulation condition is replicated 200 times to generate $r = 200$ different datasets for the following data analysis.

3.4　Data Analysis Procedure

Three methods are used to analyze each simulated dataset, including the FR method as stated in Stark et al. (2006), the B-H method as outlined in Raykov et al. (2013), and the AM method as proposed by Asparouhov & Muthén (2014). The software *Mplus* is used in the study for data analysis.

3.4.1　The FR Method

When applying the FR method, the baseline model is identified by choosing the first indicator as RI, for which the loading is set to 1 and the intercept is constrained to be equal between two groups. The latent factor mean in the reference group is set at zero and all other model parameters are free to vary. With the baseline model as a benchmark, each of the freely estimated indicator parameters is constrained in turn to form a series of nested models. Every nested model represents the hypothesis of between-group invariance of one parameter over the baseline model. This hypothesis is tested by referring to the χ^2 difference statistic. The overall α level is set at 0.05. Bonferroni's correction is used to adjust the α level for significance. If one hypothesis testing is significant at the adjusted α level, this indicator parameter is labeled as noninvariant. After completing all nested model comparisons, a list of indicators whose parameters are noninvariant become available.

3.4.2　The B-H Method

When using the B-H method, all the indicator parameters (i.e. loadings and intercepts) are constrained to be equal in the baseline model. The latent scale is identified with zero factor mean and unit variance for the reference group. The factor mean and factor variance in the focal group are freely estimated. Based on this fully constrained baseline model, a series of augmented models are created by releasing the parameter constraints one at a time. To decide whether the null hypothesis is rejected or not, each of the less constrained models is compared to the fully constrained baseline model. The difference of χ^2 values is obtained for each hypothesis testing. The p value associated with each testing is obtained through the inversion of χ^2

distribution with $df = 1$ (c.f. Bollen, 1989). Then, the B-H rejection threshold (T) is found to determine which hypothesis should be rejected. If $T = 0$, none of the null hypotheses is rejected. Otherwise, all the null hypotheses with p values that do not exceed T are rejected. The list of between-group noninvariant parameters is built according to those hypotheses with p values that did not exceed T.

3.4.3   The AM Method

When using the AM method, a two-group configural model is established first by setting zero mean and unit variance for the single latent construct in both groups. Next, this configural model undergoes an optimization process. The FREE type of alignment optimization with ML estimator is used. Then the hypothesis testing for every particular parameter is conducted by pair-wise comparison after retrieving all the parameter estimates. Three sources are referred to determine whether one parameter is noninvariant or not. The invariance hypothesis of each parameter is rejected when the p value was higher than 0.01, as recommended by Asparouhov & Muthén (2014). At the same time, the fit function contribution value (i.e. contribution of each parameter to the optimized simplicity function) and the effect size measure R^2 are also referred to make the final judgment.

3.5   Evaluation Criteria

The performance of each method is evaluated for the recovery of both the truly invariant and truly noninvariant indicator parameters embedded in each measurement model. The numbers of truly invariant and truly noninvariant parameters under different simulation conditions are displayed in Table 3.3. Three evaluation criteria are considered: 1) perfect recovery rate; 2) Type I error rate; and 3) power rate.

Table 3.3   Number of truly invariant and truly noninvariant parameters under different simulation conditions

Indicator number (P)	Modified indicator	Modified parameter(s)	Number of parameters		Percentage of noninvariant parameters
			Invariant	Noninvariant	
$P = 3$	y_1	Loading/Intercept	5	1	17%

(to be continued)

Indicator number (P)	Modified indicator	Modified parameter(s)	Number of parameters		Percentage of noninvariant parameters
			Invariant	Noninvariant	
P = 5	y_1	Loading/Intercept	9	1	10%
	y_1	Loading & Intercept	8	2	20%
	y_1, y_2	Loading/Intercept	8	2	20%
P = 7	y_1	Loading/Intercept	13	1	7%
P = 10	y_1	Loading/Intercept	19	1	5%

The perfect recovery refers to the situation that all the noninvariant parameters are correctly identified as noninvariant, and all the invariant parameters are not falsely rejected. In this study, the perfect recovery rate is calculated as the ratio of the total number of counted perfect recovery over 200 replications in each simulated condition. A perfectly recovered model has neither false positives nor false negatives. Therefore, the perfect recovery rate can be used to evaluate how well each method perfectly recovers the true invariance/noninvariance state of a population model. The perfect recovery rate can be regarded as the most rigorous form of power.

The Type I error rate is only applicable to evaluate the testing outcome of truly invariant parameters. It is computed as the average ratio between the number of falsely rejected invariant parameters and the number of truly invariant parameters in the population model. The power rate only applies to evaluate the testing outcome of truly noninvariant parameters. It is computed as the average ratio between the number of detected noninvariant parameters and the number of truly noninvariant parameters in the population model. The Type I error rate and the power rate are reported for the loading parameters and for the intercept parameters separately.

The analysis of variance (ANOVA) is conducted to determine the effects of the methods and the simulated factors (i.e. sample size, noninvariance degree, magnitude of noninvariance) on the Type I error rate and power rate. Because the sample size for the ANOVA analysis is very large, the effect size (η^2) is reported for each main factor and each interaction term. The effect size (η^2) represents the proportion of variance interpreted by each factor.

3.6　Results of the Simulation Study

For the simulation study, the testing results obtained from the three above mentioned methods (i.e. the FR method, the B-H method, and the AM method) are summarized based on the simulation design. First, in Section 3.5.1, the base Type I error rates are reported for the baseline simulation conditions without any type of measurement noninvariance. Then, for the simulation conditions with embedded noninvariance, the results are organized into three sections according to the three different ways of manipulating the magnitude of model noninvariance. In Section 3.5.2, the magnitude of noninvariance is manipulated through changing the proportion of noninvariant indicators (i.e. either one or two of the five indicators are noninvariant). In Section 3.5.3, only one of these five indicators is noninvariant. The magnitude of noninvariance is manipulated through changing this indicator from being partially noninvariant at intercept/loading to fully noninvariant at both parameters. In Section 3.5.4, the magnitude of noninvariance varies through changing the number of indicators loaded on the latent construct.

3.6.1　Baseline Data Check

In the baseline simulation condition, only the Type I error rate is examined because all the intercepts and loadings are equal between two groups. As shown in Table 3.4, all three methods show satisfactory Type I error rates on the base level, regardless of the sample size, indicator number and the tested parameter (i.e. the intercepts or loadings).

According to the analytical procedures discussed in Section 3.4, the level of significance for each method is defined differently. For the FR method, the overall α level is set at 0.05 and the level for significance is adjusted with Bonferroni's correction. Hence, under the baseline simulation condition, the nominal levels for models with different indicator numbers (i.e. $P = 3, 5, 7,$ and 10) are 0.013, 0.006, 0.004, and 0.003, respectively. The base Type I error rates given by the FR method are within or close to these nominal levels. For the B-H method, the nominal level of significance is not explicitly defined. Instead, the FDR controlling procedure is employed to control the Type I errors. The results show that the FDR controlling procedure is able to control the base Type I error rates well. For the AM method, the nominal level is preset at 0.01, following the recommendation by Asparouhov & Muthén (2014). The results show that the base Type I error rates are well confined within this nominal level.

Table 3.4   Type I error rates in the baseline conditions

Tested parameter	P	FR			B-H			AM		
		$N =$ 200	$N =$ 500	$N =$ 1000	$N =$ 200	$N =$ 500	$N =$ 1000	$N =$ 200	$N =$ 500	$N =$ 1000
Intercept	$P = 3$	0.013	0.015	0.015	0.005	0.000	0.007	0.000	0.000	0.002
	$P = 5$	0.006	0.006	0.006	0.003	0.002	0.000	0.002	0.000	0.000
	$P = 7$	0.004	0.003	0.008	0.004	0.000	0.001	0.001	0.000	0.002
	$P = 10$	0.001	0.006	0.004	0.001	0.001	0.000	0.001	0.002	0.002
Loading	$P = 3$	0.020	0.018	0.008	0.012	0.005	0.005	0.003	0.002	0.000
	$P = 5$	0.003	0.008	0.003	0.001	0.002	0.002	0.001	0.005	0.001
	$P = 7$	0.009	0.005	0.004	0.003	0.001	0.001	0.008	0.005	0.004
	$P = 10$	0.018	0.005	0.003	0.002	0.000	0.000	0.005	0.006	0.003

Note: N = sample size; P = indicator number; FR = the FR Method; B-H = the B-H method; AM = the AM method.

3.6.2   Magnitude of Noninvariance by Proportion of Noninvariant Indicators

3.6.2.1   Perfect Recovery Rate

For the perfect recovery rates, only the estimates given by the B-H method and the AM method are reported. No perfect recovery rates are reported for the FR method. This is because the first indicator y_1 is pre-fixed as the RI so that the measurement parameters located at this indicator are exempt from MI testing.

The B-H Method

As shown in Table 3.5, when using the B-H method, the perfect recovery rates are largely impacted by the proportion of noninvariant indicators.

Table 3.5　Perfect recovery rates with the B-H method when varying the proportion of noninvariant indicators

Prop	D_{inte}	Noninvariant intercepts			D_{load}	Noninvariant loadings		
		$N = 200$	$N = 500$	$N = 1000$		$N = 200$	$N = 500$	$N = 1000$
LP	$D_{\text{inte}} = 0.10$	0.020	0.050	0.170	$D_{\text{load}} = 0.05$	0.000	0.000	0.015
	$D_{\text{inte}} = 0.30$	0.340	0.620	0.395	$D_{\text{load}} = 0.15$	0.025	0.070	0.205
	$D_{\text{inte}} = 0.50$	0.515	0.070	0.000	$D_{\text{load}} = 0.25$	0.090	0.280	0.615
	$D_{\text{inte}} = 0.70$	0.170	0.000	0.000	$D_{\text{load}} = 0.35$	0.190	0.570	0.635
	$D_{\text{inte}} = 0.90$	0.005	0.000	0.000	$D_{\text{load}} = 0.45$	0.325	0.585	0.310
HP	$D_{\text{inte}} = 0.10$	0.000	0.000	0.000	$D_{\text{load}} = 0.05$	0.000	0.000	0.000
	$D_{\text{inte}} = 0.30$	0.005	0.005	0.000	$D_{\text{load}} = 0.15$	0.000	0.000	0.000
	$D_{\text{inte}} = 0.50$	0.000	0.000	0.000	$D_{\text{load}} = 0.25$	0.000	0.000	0.005
	$D_{\text{inte}} = 0.70$	0.000	0.000	0.000	$D_{\text{load}} = 0.35$	0.000	0.005	0.000
	$D_{\text{inte}} = 0.90$	0.000	0.000	0.000	$D_{\text{load}} = 0.45$	0.000	0.005	0.000

Note: Prop = Proportion; LP = low proportion; HP = high proportion; D_{inte} = degree of noninvariant intercept; D_{load} = degree of noninvariant loading; N = sample size.

Under the high proportion condition, the perfect recovery rates are either zeroes or very close to zeroes. Under the low proportion condition, the level of perfect recovery rates varies depending on the noninvariance degree and the sample size. It is found that the maximum value of perfect recovery rates tends to appear at the medium noninvariance degrees. For example, for models embedded with noninvariant intercept, the maximum value is at $D_{\text{inte}} = 0.50$ when $N = 200$, at $D_{\text{inte}} = 0.30$ when $N = 500$ or 1000. For models embedded with noninvariant loading, the maximum value is at $D_{\text{load}} = 0.35$ when $N = 1000$. Generally speaking, the maximum perfect recovery rate tends to move toward a low noninvariance degree as the sample size is large.

The AM Method

When using the AM method (as shown in Table 3.6), the perfect recovery rates are impacted by the proportion of noninvariant indicators, the sample size, and the noninvariance degree. These factors exhibit consistently either a negative effect or a positive effect on the perfect recovery rate. Specifically, the proportion of noninvariant indicators shows a negative effect: a higher proportion of noninvariant indicators reduce the perfect recovery rate. On the contrary, both the sample size and the noninvariance degree show positive effects: the larger the values of these two factors, the higher the prefect recovery rates. Additionally, conditional on the same sample size and same level of noninvariance degree, the models embedded with noninvariant intercepts are more likely to be recovered perfectly than the models embedded with noninvariant loadings.

Table 3.6   Perfect recovery rates with the AM method when varying the proportion of noninvariant indicators

Prop	D_{inte}	Noninvariant intercepts			D_{load}	Noninvariant loadings		
		$N = 200$	$N = 500$	$N = 1000$		$N = 200$	$N = 500$	$N = 1000$
LP	$D_{inte} = 0.10$	0.005	0.020	0.070	$D_{load} = 0.05$	0.000	0.000	0.005
	$D_{inte} = 0.30$	0.180	0.500	0.630	$D_{load} = 0.15$	0.005	0.035	0.190
	$D_{inte} = 0.50$	0.525	0.780	0.810	$D_{load} = 0.25$	0.030	0.180	0.625
	$D_{inte} = 0.70$	0.735	0.870	0.880	$D_{load} = 0.35$	0.075	0.490	0.910
	$D_{inte} = 0.90$	0.810	0.875	0.925	$D_{load} = 0.45$	0.135	0.725	0.975
HP	$D_{inte} = 0.10$	0.000	0.005	0.000	$D_{load} = 0.05$	0.000	0.000	0.000
	$D_{inte} = 0.30$	0.015	0.130	0.265	$D_{load} = 0.15$	0.000	0.000	0.020
	$D_{inte} = 0.50$	0.115	0.320	0.385	$D_{load} = 0.25$	0.000	0.025	0.255
	$D_{inte} = 0.70$	0.255	0.400	0.450	$D_{load} = 0.35$	0.010	0.170	0.655
	$D_{inte} = 0.90$	0.320	0.460	0.510	$D_{load} = 0.45$	0.070	0.440	0.850

Note: Prop = Proportion; LP = low proportion; HP = high proportion; D_{inte} = degree of noninvariant intercept; D_{load} = degree of noninvariant loading; N = sample size.

Comparison of Perfect Recovery Rates Between the B-H Method and the AM Method

In Figure 3.1 and Figure 3.2, the perfect recovery rates estimated by the B-H method and the AM method are compared. Figure 3.1 described the situation when the noninvariance is located at the intercepts. Figure 3.2 described the situation when the noninvariance is located at the loadings.

According to these two figures, the B-H method and the AM method are impacted differently by the three simulation factors (i.e. the proportion of noninvariant indicators, the sample size and the noninvariance degree).

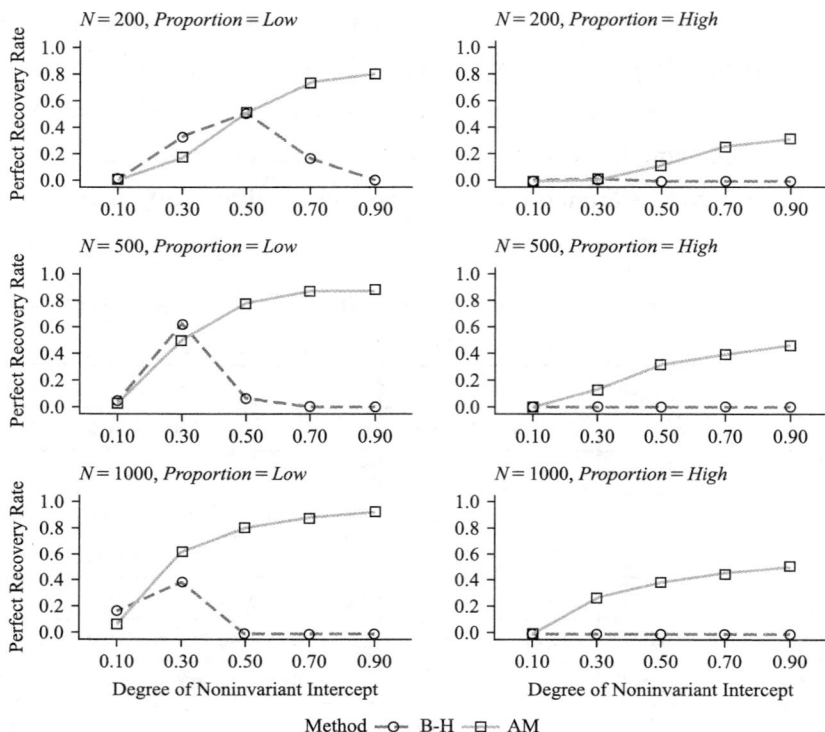

Figure 3.1   Perfect recovery rates for models with noninvariance in the intercepts when varying the proportion of noninvariant indicators

First, the B-H method is more affected by increasing the proportion of noninvariant indicators than the AM method. Under the high proportion condition, the perfect recovery rates estimated by the B-H method are reduced to zeroes in most simulation cases. The AM method, however, performs well under some restricted conditions (i.e. the perfect recovery rates are high if the noninvariance degree and the sample size are large). Second, the sample size effect is different. For the B-H method, as the sample size becomes large, the maximum recovery rate moves toward small noninvariance degrees. If the AM method is employed, the perfect recovery rate is consistently enhanced by larger sample sizes. Third, two methods perform differently with regard to the relationship between the perfect recovery rate and the noninvariance degree. For the B-H method, the perfect recovery rate is not uniformly increased by large noninvariance degrees. For the AM method, the perfect recovery

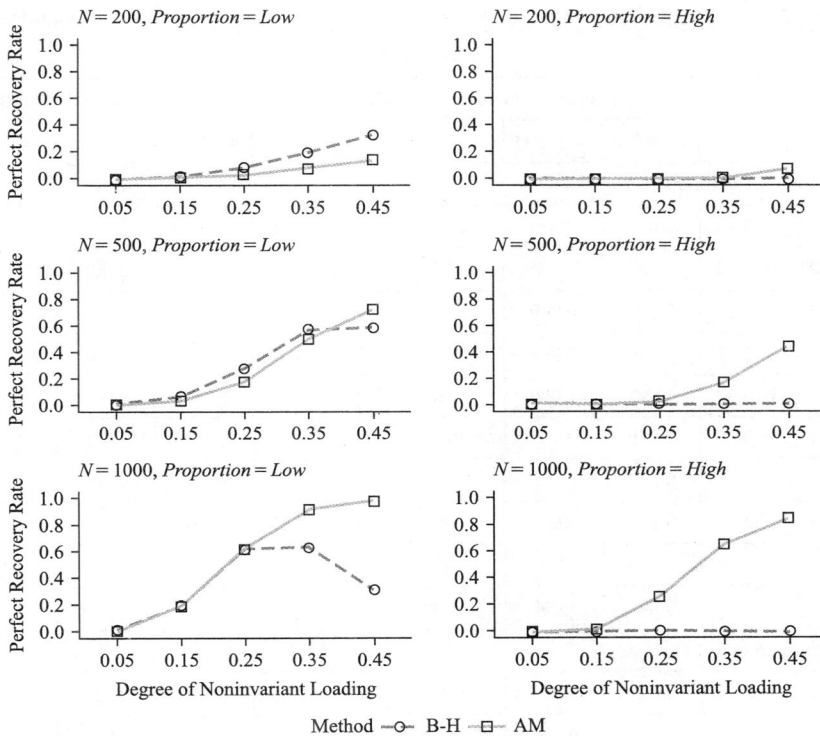

Figure 3.2   Perfect recovery rates for models with noninvariance in the loadings when varying the proportion of noninvariant indicators

rate is consistently increased by large noninvariance degrees under all simulation conditions.

3.6.2.2   Type I Error Rate

The Type I error rate represents the average value of false positive (i.e. incorrect findings of truly invariant parameters as noninvariant) across replicates. In this study, the Type I error rates for testing the truly invariant intercepts and the truly invariant loadings are reported separately.

The FR Method

The Type I error rates estimated by the FR method are presented in Table 3.7.

Table 3.7　Type I error rates with the FR method when varying the proportion of noninvariant indicators

Prop	D_{inte}	Noninvariant intercepts			D_{load}	Noninvariant loadings		
		$N = 200$	$N = 500$	$N = 1000$		$N = 200$	$N = 500$	$N = 1000$
Testing truly invariant intercepts								
LP	$D_{\text{inte}} = 0.10$	0.029	0.064	0.133	$D_{\text{load}} = 0.05$	0.008	0.006	0.006
	$D_{\text{inte}} = 0.30$	0.228	0.601	0.929	$D_{\text{load}} = 0.15$	0.009	0.005	0.006
	$D_{\text{inte}} = 0.50$	0.540	0.949	1.000	$D_{\text{load}} = 0.25$	0.010	0.004	0.005
	$D_{\text{inte}} = 0.70$	0.784	0.998	1.000	$D_{\text{load}} = 0.35$	0.009	0.005	0.005
	$D_{\text{inte}} = 0.90$	0.893	1.000	1.000	$D_{\text{load}} = 0.45$	0.008	0.005	0.006
HP	$D_{\text{inte}} = 0.10$	0.030	0.067	0.132	$D_{\text{load}} = 0.05$	0.008	0.006	0.006
	$D_{\text{inte}} = 0.30$	0.237	0.595	0.930	$D_{\text{load}} = 0.15$	0.011	0.006	0.006
	$D_{\text{inte}} = 0.50$	0.553	0.955	1.000	$D_{\text{load}} = 0.25$	0.010	0.005	0.005
	$D_{\text{inte}} = 0.70$	0.780	1.000	1.000	$D_{\text{load}} = 0.35$	0.009	0.005	0.005
	$D_{\text{inte}} = 0.90$	0.895	1.000	1.000	$D_{\text{load}} = 0.45$	0.008	0.005	0.004
Testing truly invariant loadings								
LP	$D_{\text{inte}} = 0.10$	0.003	0.008	0.003	$D_{\text{load}} = 0.05$	0.005	0.011	0.015
	$D_{\text{inte}} = 0.30$	0.003	0.008	0.003	$D_{\text{load}} = 0.15$	0.024	0.073	0.170
	$D_{\text{inte}} = 0.50$	0.003	0.008	0.003	$D_{\text{load}} = 0.25$	0.074	0.214	0.514
	$D_{\text{inte}} = 0.70$	0.003	0.008	0.003	$D_{\text{load}} = 0.35$	0.143	0.461	0.841
	$D_{\text{inte}} = 0.90$	0.003	0.008	0.003	$D_{\text{load}} = 0.45$	0.239	0.698	0.969
HP	$D_{\text{inte}} = 0.10$	0.003	0.008	0.003	$D_{\text{load}} = 0.05$	0.005	0.010	0.013
	$D_{\text{inte}} = 0.30$	0.003	0.008	0.003	$D_{\text{load}} = 0.15$	0.030	0.073	0.183
	$D_{\text{inte}} = 0.50$	0.003	0.008	0.003	$D_{\text{load}} = 0.25$	0.082	0.235	0.555
	$D_{\text{inte}} = 0.70$	0.003	0.008	0.003	$D_{\text{load}} = 0.35$	0.158	0.502	0.863
	$D_{\text{inte}} = 0.90$	0.003	0.008	0.003	$D_{\text{load}} = 0.45$	0.263	0.758	0.978

Note: Prop = Proportion; LP = low proportion; HP = high proportion; D_{inte} = degree of noninvariant intercept; D_{load} = degree of noninvariant loading; N = sample size.

It shows that the existence of noninvariant intercepts/loadings does not largely affect the Type I errors on testing the other type of parameters. To be more specific, the testing of truly invariant loadings is not largely affected by the noninvariant intercepts, and the testing of truly invariant intercepts is not largely affected by the noninvariant loadings. On the contrary, the existence of noninvariant intercepts/ loadings does impact the testing outcomes for the same type of truly invariant parameters. In such cases, the Type I error rate increases with the increase of sample size, the noninvariance degree, and the proportion of noninvariant indicators. Namely, the larger value of these three simulated factors, the more likely the truly invariant intercepts/loadings will be wrongly rejected.

The B-H Method

As indicated in Table 3.8, the existence of noninvariant intercepts/loadings impacts the Type I error rates for both types of parameters. To be more specific, the existence of noninvariant intercepts not only leads to more Type I errors for testing the intercepts, but also leads to more Type I errors for testing the loadings. Similarly, the existence of noninvariant loadings also causes more Type I errors when testing both the loadings and intercepts. In addition, all three simulation factors (i.e. sample size, noninvariance degree, and proportion of noninvariant indicators) are positively related to the Type I error rate. That is, larger values of these three factors correspond to more severe Type I error rates. Moreover, it is observed that the Type I error rates are always higher for models contaminated by noninvariant intercepts than those contaminated by noninvariant loadings, conditional on the same level of other simulation factors.

Table 3.8   Type I error rates with the B-H method when varying the proportion of noninvariant indicators

Prop	D_{inte}	Noninvariant intercepts			D_{load}	Noninvariant loadings		
		$N = 200$	$N = 500$	$N = 1000$		$N = 200$	$N = 500$	$N = 1000$
Testing truly invariant intercepts								
LP	$D_{inte} = 0.10$	0.004	0.006	0.133	$D_{load} = 0.05$	0.004	0.002	0.000
	$D_{inte} = 0.30$	0.021	0.055	0.929	$D_{load} = 0.15$	0.003	0.005	0.001
	$D_{inte} = 0.50$	0.090	0.353	1.000	$D_{load} = 0.25$	0.005	0.010	0.011
	$D_{inte} = 0.70$	0.283	0.793	1.000	$D_{load} = 0.35$	0.009	0.017	0.027
	$D_{inte} = 0.90$	0.555	0.970	1.000	$D_{load} = 0.45$	0.009	0.028	0.055

(*to be continued*)

Prop	D_{inte}	Noninvariant intercepts			D_{load}	Noninvariant loadings		
		$N = 200$	$N = 500$	$N = 1000$		$N = 200$	$N = 500$	$N = 1000$
HP	$D_{\text{inte}} = 0.10$	0.005	0.012	0.132	$D_{\text{load}} = 0.05$	0.003	0.002	0.001
	$D_{\text{inte}} = 0.30$	0.083	0.350	0.930	$D_{\text{load}} = 0.15$	0.004	0.005	0.004
	$D_{\text{inte}} = 0.50$	0.417	0.912	1.000	$D_{\text{load}} = 0.25$	0.002	0.008	0.018
	$D_{\text{inte}} = 0.70$	0.785	0.998	1.000	$D_{\text{load}} = 0.35$	0.003	0.015	0.025
	$D_{\text{inte}} = 0.90$	0.933	1.000	1.000	$D_{\text{load}} = 0.45$	0.005	0.019	0.030
Testing truly invariant loadings								
LP	$D_{\text{inte}} = 0.10$	0.001	0.006	0.004	$D_{\text{load}} = 0.05$	0.001	0.004	0.001
	$D_{\text{inte}} = 0.30$	0.012	0.039	0.079	$D_{\text{load}} = 0.15$	0.001	0.008	0.006
	$D_{\text{inte}} = 0.50$	0.070	0.200	0.293	$D_{\text{load}} = 0.25$	0.008	0.016	0.034
	$D_{\text{inte}} = 0.70$	0.175	0.357	0.567	$D_{\text{load}} = 0.35$	0.014	0.041	0.081
	$D_{\text{inte}} = 0.90$	0.302	0.594	0.878	$D_{\text{load}} = 0.45$	0.024	0.073	0.210
HP	$D_{\text{inte}} = 0.10$	0.001	0.004	0.007	$D_{\text{load}} = 0.05$	0.002	0.005	0.002
	$D_{\text{inte}} = 0.30$	0.015	0.061	0.179	$D_{\text{load}} = 0.15$	0.008	0.015	0.035
	$D_{\text{inte}} = 0.50$	0.105	0.369	0.707	$D_{\text{load}} = 0.25$	0.015	0.070	0.232
	$D_{\text{inte}} = 0.70$	0.271	0.741	0.966	$D_{\text{load}} = 0.35$	0.033	0.210	0.582
	$D_{\text{inte}} = 0.90$	0.464	0.908	0.999	$D_{\text{load}} = 0.45$	0.075	0.432	0.850

Note: Prop = Proportion; LP = low proportion; HP = high proportion; D_{inte} =degree of noninvariant intercept; D_{load} = degree of noninvariant loading; N = sample size.

The AM Method

The AM method performs well in controlling the Type I error rates. As shown in Table 3.9, no matter whether the truly invariant intercepts or loadings are tested, the Type I error rates are zeroes or close to zeroes in most simulation conditions. The Type I errors are relatively high only at some extreme simulation conditions (e.g. testing the truly invariant loadings under the HP condition and $D_{\text{load}} \geqslant 0.15$).

Comparison of Type I Error Rates Among the Three Methods

First, three methods are compared for the Type I error rates of testing the truly invariant intercepts. Figure 3.3 and Figure 3.4 compare three methods when the noninvariance is located at the intercepts or loadings respectively.

Table 3.9　Type I error rates with the AM method when varying the proportion of noninvariant indicators

Prop	D_{inte}	Noninvariant intercepts			D_{load}	Noninvariant loadings		
		$N = 200$	$N = 500$	$N = 1000$		$N = 200$	$N = 500$	$N = 1000$
Testing truly invariant intercepts								
LP	$D_{inte} = 0.10$	0.001	0.000	0.000	$D_{load} = 0.05$	0.001	0.000	0.000
	$D_{inte} = 0.30$	0.000	0.000	0.000	$D_{load} = 0.15$	0.003	0.000	0.000
	$D_{inte} = 0.50$	0.000	0.000	0.000	$D_{load} = 0.25$	0.003	0.000	0.001
	$D_{inte} = 0.70$	0.000	0.000	0.000	$D_{load} = 0.35$	0.002	0.001	0.002
	$D_{inte} = 0.90$	0.000	0.000	0.000	$D_{load} = 0.45$	0.003	0.001	0.002
HP	$D_{inte} = 0.10$	0.002	0.000	0.000	$D_{load} = 0.05$	0.001	0.001	0.000
	$D_{inte} = 0.30$	0.002	0.003	0.000	$D_{load} = 0.15$	0.001	0.001	0.000
	$D_{inte} = 0.50$	0.000	0.003	0.002	$D_{load} = 0.25$	0.002	0.001	0.000
	$D_{inte} = 0.70$	0.000	0.003	0.000	$D_{load} = 0.35$	0.002	0.001	0.001
	$D_{inte} = 0.90$	0.002	0.003	0.000	$D_{load} = 0.45$	0.003	0.002	0.001
Testing truly invariant loadings								
LP	$D_{inte} = 0.10$	0.001	0.005	0.001	$D_{load} = 0.05$	0.001	0.005	0.001
	$D_{inte} = 0.30$	0.001	0.005	0.001	$D_{load} = 0.15$	0.001	0.006	0.004
	$D_{inte} = 0.50$	0.001	0.005	0.001	$D_{load} = 0.25$	0.004	0.006	0.004
	$D_{inte} = 0.70$	0.001	0.005	0.001	$D_{load} = 0.35$	0.003	0.005	0.003
	$D_{inte} = 0.90$	0.001	0.005	0.001	$D_{load} = 0.45$	0.001	0.005	0.003
HP	$D_{inte} = 0.10$	0.001	0.005	0.001	$D_{load} = 0.05$	0.002	0.005	0.002
	$D_{inte} = 0.30$	0.001	0.005	0.001	$D_{load} = 0.15$	0.007	0.015	0.020
	$D_{inte} = 0.50$	0.001	0.005	0.001	$D_{load} = 0.25$	0.010	0.020	0.018
	$D_{inte} = 0.70$	0.001	0.005	0.001	$D_{load} = 0.35$	0.013	0.018	0.012
	$D_{inte} = 0.90$	0.001	0.005	0.001	$D_{load} = 0.45$	0.015	0.020	0.015

Note: Prop = Proportion; LP = low proportion; HP = high proportion; D_{inte} = degree of noninvariant intercept; D_{load} = degree of noninvariant loading; N = sample size.

As shown in Figure 3.3, with noninvariant intercepts, the AM method performs much better than the other two methods. The AM method has zero or close to zero Type I error rates under all simulation conditions. In contrast, both the FR method and the B-H method are affected by the sample size, the noninvariance degree, and the proportion of noninvariant indicators. Comparatively speaking, the B-H method performs better than the FR method under the majority of simulation conditions. The B-H method is better at controlling Type I errors than the FR method under the conditions of small sample size, medium noninvariance degree, and low proportion of noninvariant indicators.

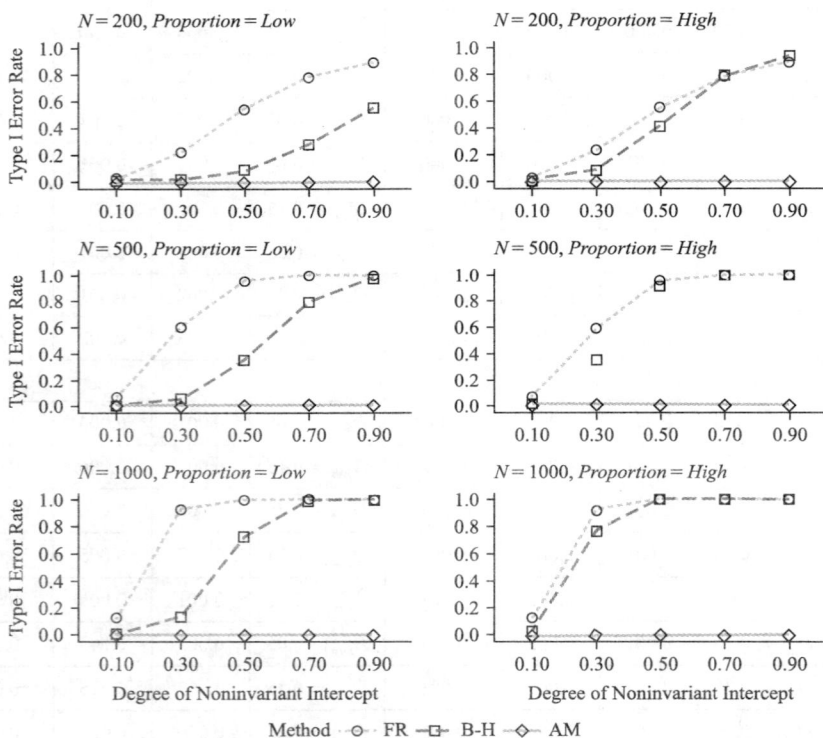

Figure 3.3   Type I error rates of testing intercepts for models with noninvariance in the intercepts when varying the proportion of noninvariant indicators

As shown in Figure 3.4, when the noninvariance is located at the loadings, all three methods report low Type I error rates. Particularly for the FR method and the AM method, the Type I error rates are close to zeroes under all simulation conditions. For the B-H method, the Type I error rates increase slightly under the conditions of larger sample size and noninvariance degrees (e.g. $N = 1000$ and $D_{load} \geqslant 0.35$).

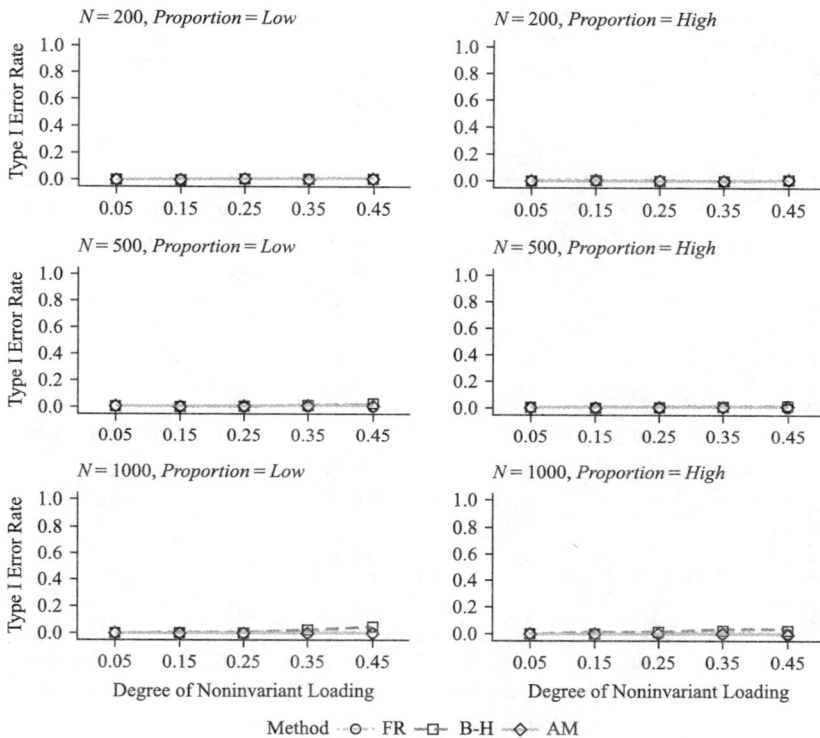

Figure 3.4   Type I error rates of testing intercepts for models with noninvariance in the loadings when varying the proportion of noninvariant indicators

Second, three methods are also compared for the Type I error rates of testing the truly invariant loadings (see Figure 3.5 and Figure 3.6). As shown in Figure 3.5, when noninvariant intercepts exist in the models, both the FR method and the AM method perform well. The Type I errors generated by these two methods are always low. The B-H method, however, does not perform quite well, particularly when the sample size and the noninvariance degree are large.

As shown in Figure 3.6, when the noninvariance is located at the loadings, the AM method still performs quite well and is the best method. The FR method, however, becomes the worst method. It always reports larger Type I errors than the other two methods. The B-H method is better than the FR method, but worse than the AM method. Unlike the AM method, which is not affected by any simulation conditions, the performances of the other two methods are compromised by large sample

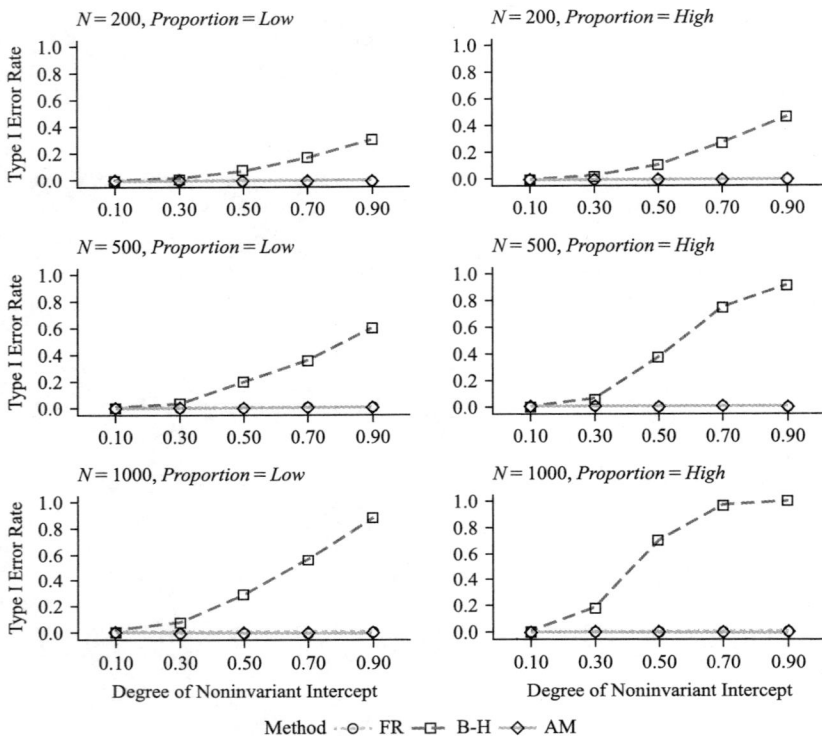

Figure 3.5　Type I error rates of testing loadings for models with noninvariance in the intercepts
when varying the proportion of noninvariant indicators

size, large noninvariance degree, and high proportion of noninvariant indicators.

3.6.2.3　Power Rate

The power rate represents the average value of true negative (i.e. the correct justification of truly noninvariant parameters as noninvariant) across replicates. The testing results of truly noninvariant intercepts and truly noninvariant loadings are reported separately.

The FR Method

When choosing the FR method, no power rates are reported for the low proportion condition. Under the high proportion condition, the power rates are calculated for detecting the parameters located at the indicator y_2. As shown in Table 3.10, the FR method has no enough power to correctly identify the truly noninvariant intercepts/loadings in the models. The general loss of power suggests that the fixation

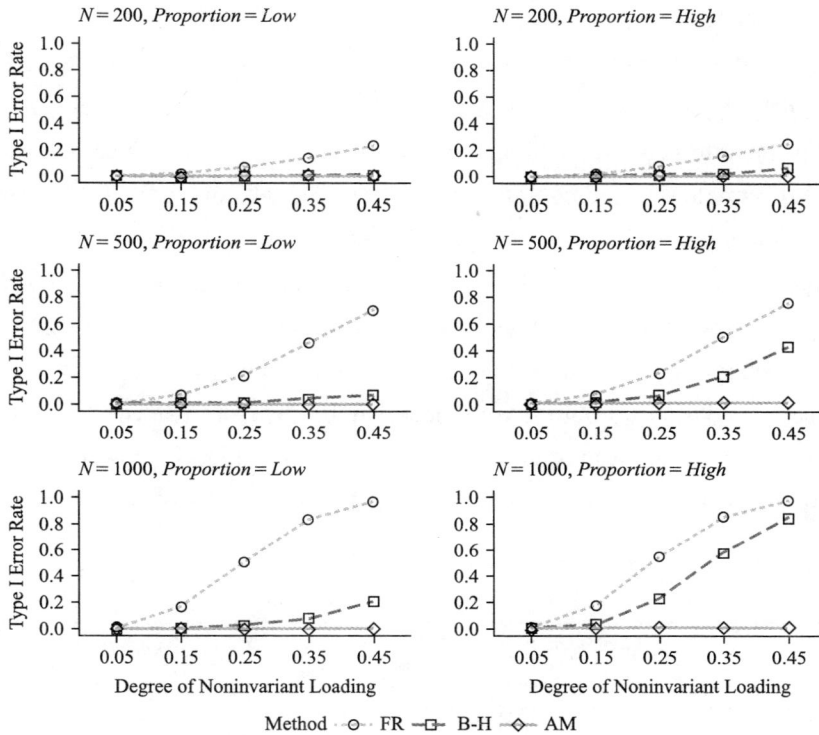

Figure 3.6   Type I error rates of testing loadings for models with noninvariance in the loadings when varying the proportion of noninvariant indicators

of noninvariant y_1 as an RI has large negative effect on detecting measurement noninvariance in the models.

Table 3.10   Power rates with the FR method when varying the proportion of noninvariant indicators

Prop	D_{inte}	Noninvariant intercepts			D_{load}	Noninvariant loadings		
		$N = 200$	$N = 500$	$N = 1000$		$N = 200$	$N = 500$	$N = 1000$
HP	$D_{inte} = 0.10$	0.000	0.010	0.005	$D_{load} = 0.05$	0.000	0.010	0.000
	$D_{inte} = 0.30$	0.010	0.005	0.005	$D_{load} = 0.15$	0.000	0.010	0.005
	$D_{inte} = 0.50$	0.015	0.010	0.005	$D_{load} = 0.25$	0.000	0.005	0.010
	$D_{inte} = 0.70$	0.015	0.005	0.005	$D_{load} = 0.35$	0.000	0.005	0.010
	$D_{inte} = 0.90$	0.015	0.005	0.010	$D_{load} = 0.45$	0.000	0.005	0.010

Note: Prop = Proportion; HP = high proportion; D_{inte} = degree of noninvariant intercept; D_{load} = degree of noninvariant loading; N = sample size.

The B-H Method

Unlike the FR method, all the truly noninvariant parameters are tested when choosing the B-H method. As shown in Table 3.11, no matter whether the truly noninvariant intercepts or loadings are tested, the power rates increase with the increase of sample size and noninvariance degree. On the contrary, a high proportion of noninvariant indicators reduce the power rates.

In addition, the B-H method is more powerful in detecting the truly noninvariant intercepts than detecting the truly noninvariant loadings. For example, conditional on the largest sample size (i.e. $N = 1000$) and low proportion of noninvariant indicators, the power rate during testing the truly noninvariant intercept reaches one at $D_{\text{inte}} \geqslant$ 0.30. In contrast, when testing the truly noninvariant loading, the power rate reaches one only at the highest degree of noninvariance (i.e. $D_{\text{load}} = 0.45$).

Table 3.11　Power rates with the B-H method when varying the proportion of noninvariant indicators

Prop	D_{inte}	Noninvariant intercepts			D_{load}	Noninvariant loadings		
		$N = 200$	$N = 500$	$N = 1000$		$N = 200$	$N = 500$	$N = 1000$
LP	$D_{\text{inte}} = 0.10$	0.020	0.080	0.185	$D_{\text{load}} = 0.05$	0.000	0.000	0.015
	$D_{\text{inte}} = 0.30$	0.445	0.940	1.000	$D_{\text{load}} = 0.15$	0.025	0.085	0.225
	$D_{\text{inte}} = 0.50$	0.965	1.000	1.000	$D_{\text{load}} = 0.25$	0.105	0.370	0.775
	$D_{\text{inte}} = 0.70$	1.000	1.000	1.000	$D_{\text{load}} = 0.35$	0.240	0.775	0.990
	$D_{\text{inte}} = 0.90$	1.000	1.000	1.000	$D_{\text{load}} = 0.45$	0.450	0.910	1.000
HP	$D_{\text{inte}} = 0.10$	0.003	0.025	0.060	$D_{\text{load}} = 0.05$	0.000	0.000	0.005
	$D_{\text{inte}} = 0.30$	0.185	0.568	0.948	$D_{\text{load}} = 0.15$	0.010	0.015	0.078
	$D_{\text{inte}} = 0.50$	0.543	0.965	1.000	$D_{\text{load}} = 0.25$	0.025	0.123	0.403
	$D_{\text{inte}} = 0.70$	0.750	0.998	1.000	$D_{\text{load}} = 0.35$	0.083	0.325	0.768
	$D_{\text{inte}} = 0.90$	0.830	1.000	1.000	$D_{\text{load}} = 0.45$	0.140	0.568	0.915

Note: Prop = Proportion; LP = low proportion; HP = high proportion; D_{inte} = degree of noninvariant intercept; D_{load} = degree of noninvariant loading; N = sample size.

The AM Method

For the AM method, all the noninvariant parameters in the models are available for testing as well. As shown in Table 3.12, no matter whether the truly noninvariant intercepts or loadings are tested, the power rates increase with the increase of sample size and noninvariance degree. On the contrary, the proportion of noninvariant indicators exhibit negative effects: a high proportion of noninvariant indicators leads to lower power rates.

Additionally, the AM method is more sensitive in detecting the noninvariant intercepts than detecting the noninvariant loadings under the majority of simulation conditions. Only at some extreme conditions (e.g. $N = 1000$, $D_{load} \geq 0.35$), the power rates for detecting the noninvariant loadings are higher.

Table 3.12   Power rates with the AM method when varying the proportion of noninvariant indicators

Prop	D_{inte}	Noninvariant intercepts			D_{load}	Noninvariant loadings		
		$N = 200$	$N = 500$	$N = 1000$		$N = 200$	$N = 500$	$N = 1000$
LP	$D_{inte} = 0.10$	0.005	0.020	0.070	$D_{load} = 0.05$	0.000	0.000	0.005
	$D_{inte} = 0.30$	0.185	0.510	0.630	$D_{load} = 0.15$	0.005	0.035	0.190
	$D_{inte} = 0.50$	0.530	0.790	0.810	$D_{load} = 0.25$	0.030	0.180	0.625
	$D_{inte} = 0.70$	0.740	0.885	0.880	$D_{load} = 0.35$	0.075	0.495	0.930
	$D_{inte} = 0.90$	0.815	0.890	0.930	$D_{load} = 0.45$	0.135	0.740	0.995
HP	$D_{inte} = 0.10$	0.000	0.008	0.010	$D_{load} = 0.05$	0.000	0.003	0.000
	$D_{inte} = 0.30$	0.053	0.195	0.338	$D_{load} = 0.15$	0.000	0.020	0.073
	$D_{inte} = 0.50$	0.175	0.368	0.423	$D_{load} = 0.25$	0.010	0.090	0.378
	$D_{inte} = 0.70$	0.300	0.428	0.475	$D_{load} = 0.35$	0.043	0.293	0.735
	$D_{inte} = 0.90$	0.345	0.488	0.540	$D_{load} = 0.45$	0.110	0.558	0.925

Note: Prop = Proportion; LP = low proportion; HP = high proportion; D_{inte} = degree of noninvariant intercept; D_{load} = degree of noninvariant loading; N = sample size.

Comparison of Power Rates Among the Three Methods

First, the power rates of identifying the noninvariant intercepts are compared among the three methods (as shown in Figure 3.7). Under the low proportion condition, only the results from the B-H method and the AM method are available for comparison. The FR method is not available because the indicator y_1 is initially set as an RI. Under the high proportion condition, all three methods are available for comparison.

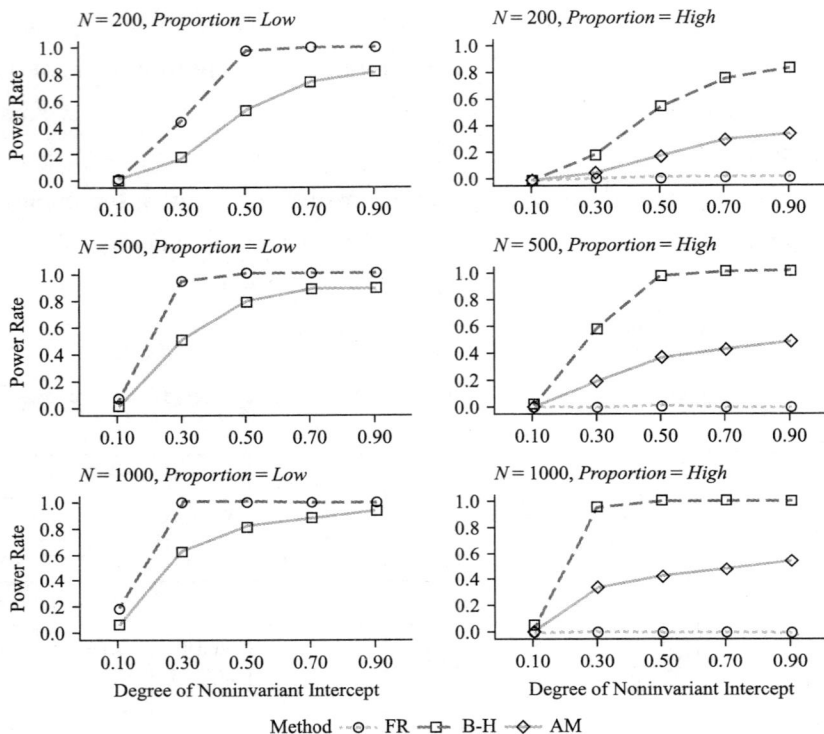

Figure 3.7   Power rates of testing intercepts when varying the proportion of noninvariant indicators

In both the low and high proportion conditions, the B-H method performs better than the AM method. As to the FR method, unlike the previous two methods, it always performs the worst and does not have powers to detect noninvariant intercepts under all conditions.

Second, the power rates of identifying the noninvariant loadings by the three methods are compared, as shown in Figure 3.8.

It is observed that under the low proportion condition, the B-H method always performs better than the AM method, regardless of the sample size and noninvariance degree. The existence of high proportion of noninvariant loadings negatively impacts both the B-H method and the AM method. The B-H method is still slightly better than the AM method under most simulation conditions. The FR method performs the worst among the three methods. This method is unable to correctly identify the noninvariant loadings and the power rates are always zeroes or close to zeroes.

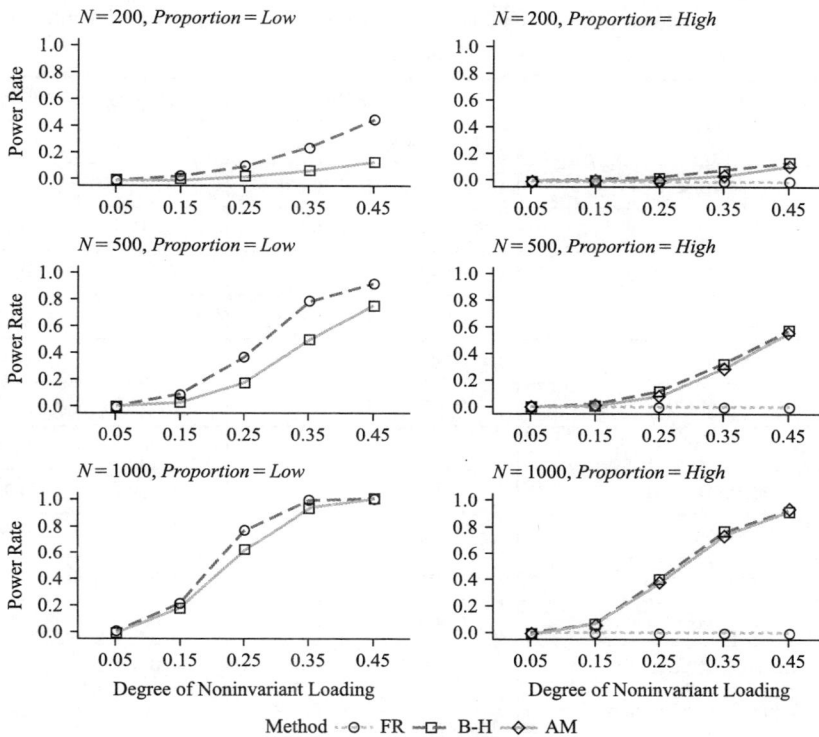

Figure 3.8   Power rates of testing loadings when varying the proportion of noninvariant indicators

3.6.2.4   Design Effects

An analysis of variance test is conducted to evaluate whether the three different methods and the simulation factors (i.e. sample size, noninvariance degree, and proportion of noninvariant indicators) have any effect on the Type I error rates and power rates. Table 3.13 presents the effect sizes (η^2) of all the main factors and interaction terms.The results show that the two main factors (i.e. the method and noninvariance degree) interpret more variation of both the Type I error rate and power rate than the other factors.

3.6.3   Magnitude of Noninvariance at the Same Indicator

In this section, rather than increasing the proportion of noninvariant indicators as described in the previous section, the magnitude of model noninvariance varies at the same indicator which is either partially or fully noninvariant.

Table 3.13　Effect size (η^2) of design factors when varying the proportion of noninvariant indicators

Design Factor	Type I Error Rate		Power Rate	
	Intercept	Loading	Intercept	Loading
Method	0.150	0.098	0.378	0.129
N	0.016	0.053	0.017	0.096
D	0.088	0.136	0.163	0.175
Proportion	0.002	0.009	0.021	0.012
Method*N	0.008	0.027	0.009	0.047
Method*D	0.048	0.075	0.093	0.089
N*D	0.006	0.030	0.009	0.053
Method* Proportion	0.005	0.014	0.018	0.009
N* Proportion	0.000	0.003	0.001	0.001
D* Proportion	0.001	0.005	0.003	0.005
Method*N*D	0.005	0.016	0.007	0.028
Method*N*Proportion	0.000	0.005	0.002	0.001
Method*D*Proportion	0.002	0.009	0.007	0.003
N*D* Proportion	0.001	0.002	0.002	0.003
Method*N*D* Proportion	0.003	0.003	0.002	0.002

Note: N = sample size; D = degree of noninvariant parameter.

3.6.3.1　Perfect Recovery Rate

　　Table 3.14 reports the perfect recovery rates when both the intercept and loading at the same indicator are noninvariant. No perfect recovery rate is reported for the FR method due to the RI setting. For the B-H method, the maximum value of perfect recovery rate appears at the medium noninvariance degree. For the AM method, the maximum value appears at the largest noninvariance degree.

Table 3.14　Perfect recovery rates with both noninvariant parameters at the same indicator

Method	D_{inte} & D_{load}	$N = 200$	$N = 500$	$N = 1000$
	$D_{inte} = 0.10$ & $D_{load} = 0.05$	0.000	0.000	0.035
	$D_{inte} = 0.30$ & $D_{load} = 0.15$	0.130	0.320	0.170

(to be continued)

Method	D_{inte} & D_{load}	$N = 200$	$N = 500$	$N = 1000$
B-H	$D_{inte} = 0.50$ & $D_{load} = 0.25$	0.215	0.020	0.000
	$D_{inte} = 0.70$ & $D_{load} = 0.35$	0.110	0.000	0.000
	$D_{inte} = 0.90$ & $D_{load} = 0.45$	0.060	0.000	0.000
AM	$D_{inte} = 0.10$ & $D_{load} = 0.05$	0.000	0.000	0.000
	$D_{inte} = 0.30$ & $D_{load} = 0.15$	0.000	0.000	0.000
	$D_{inte} = 0.50$ & $D_{load} = 0.25$	0.000	0.010	0.010
	$D_{inte} = 0.70$ & $D_{load} = 0.35$	0.000	0.010	0.060
	$D_{inte} = 0.90$ & $D_{load} = 0.45$	0.010	0.030	0.085

Note: D_{inte} = degree of noninvariant intercept; D_{load} = degree of noninvariant loading; N = sample size.

To evaluate the effect after modifying a partially noninvariant indicator to be fully noninvariant, the change of perfect recovery rate is compared. In Figure 3.9, two partially noninvariant conditions (i.e. models with a single noninvariant intercept/ loading) are compared with the fully noninvariant condition (i.e. models with both noninvariant intercept and loading).

First, in contrast to the models contaminated by a single noninvariant intercept, the perfect recovery rates obtained from both the B-H method and the AM method are reduced under the fully noninvariant condition.

Second, compared to the models contaminated by a single noninvariant loading, the AM method is consistently compromised under the fully noninvariant condition. The perfect recovery rates are reduced as the sample size and the noninvariance degree increased. Yet, for the B-H method, the perfect recovery rates tend to be negatively impacted at large noninvariance degrees, but positively impacted at low noninvariance degrees.

3.6.3.2   Type I Error Rate

Table 3.15 and Table 3.16 report the Type I error rates of testing the intercepts and loadings when both parameters at the same indicator are noninvariant. As shown in these two tables, no matter whether the intercepts/loadings are tested, the AM method is not impacted by any simulation condition. The Type I error rates are zeroes or near to zeros. Yet, for the FR method and the B-H method, the Type I error rates increase as the sample size and the noninvariance degree increase.

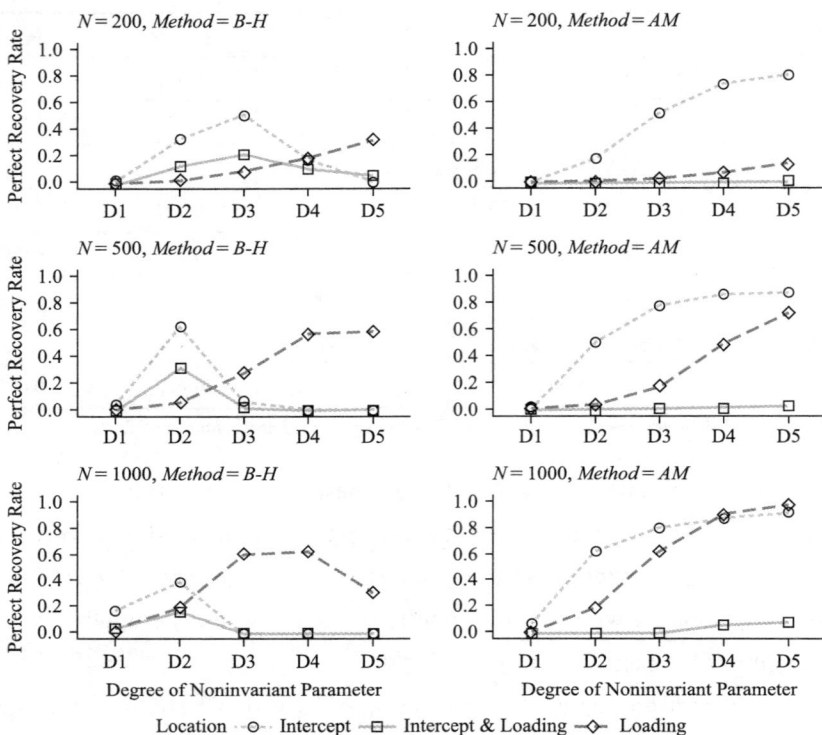

Figure 3.9[①]   Perfect recovery rates with the variation of noninvariance at the same indicator

Table 3.15   Type I error rates of testing intercepts with both noninvariant parameters at the same indicator

Method	D_{inte} & D_{load}	$N = 200$	$N = 500$	$N = 1000$
FR	$D_{inte} = 0.10$ & $D_{load} = 0.05$	0.026	0.061	0.118
	$D_{inte} = 0.30$ & $D_{load} = 0.15$	0.171	0.463	0.810
	$D_{inte} = 0.50$ & $D_{load} = 0.25$	0.346	0.809	0.988
	$D_{inte} = 0.70$ & $D_{load} = 0.35$	0.529	0.944	1.000
	$D_{inte} = 0.90$ & $D_{load} = 0.45$	0.650	0.983	1.000

(*to be continued*)

---

① In this figure, D1-D5 represent the noninvariance condition for the intercept or/and loading from the smallest to the largest degree, i.e. D1 denotes the condition of $D_{inte} = 0.10$ or/and $D_{load} = 0.05$.

Method	D_{inte} & D_{load}	$N = 200$	$N = 500$	$N = 1000$
B-H	$D_{inte} = 0.10$ & $D_{load} = 0.05$	0.004	0.009	0.005
	$D_{inte} = 0.30$ & $D_{load} = 0.15$	0.034	0.119	0.271
	$D_{inte} = 0.50$ & $D_{load} = 0.25$	0.161	0.546	0.910
	$D_{inte} = 0.70$ & $D_{load} = 0.35$	0.370	0.869	0.999
	$D_{inte} = 0.90$ & $D_{load} = 0.45$	0.499	0.936	1.000
AM	$D_{inte} = 0.10$ & $D_{load} = 0.05$	0.001	0.000	0.000
	$D_{inte} = 0.30$ & $D_{load} = 0.15$	0.000	0.000	0.001
	$D_{inte} = 0.50$ & $D_{load} = 0.25$	0.000	0.000	0.001
	$D_{inte} = 0.70$ & $D_{load} = 0.35$	0.001	0.000	0.003
	$D_{inte} = 0.90$ & $D_{load} = 0.45$	0.003	0.000	0.004

Note: D_{inte} = degree of noninvariant intercept; D_{load} = degree of noninvariant loading; N = sample size.

Table 3.16　Type I error rates of testing loadings with both noninvariant parameters at the same indicator

Method	D_{inte} & D_{load}	$N = 200$	$N = 500$	$N = 1000$
FR	$D_{inte} = 0.10$ & $D_{load} = 0.05$	0.005	0.011	0.015
	$D_{inte} = 0.30$ & $D_{load} = 0.15$	0.024	0.073	0.170
	$D_{inte} = 0.50$ & $D_{load} = 0.25$	0.074	0.214	0.514
	$D_{inte} = 0.70$ & $D_{load} = 0.35$	0.143	0.461	0.841
	$D_{inte} = 0.90$ & $D_{load} = 0.45$	0.239	0.698	0.969
B-H	$D_{inte} = 0.10$ & $D_{load} = 0.05$	0.001	0.006	0.004
	$D_{inte} = 0.30$ & $D_{load} = 0.15$	0.015	0.050	0.099
	$D_{inte} = 0.50$ & $D_{load} = 0.25$	0.051	0.223	0.535
	$D_{inte} = 0.70$ & $D_{load} = 0.35$	0.123	0.513	0.855
	$D_{inte} = 0.90$ & $D_{load} = 0.45$	0.153	0.581	0.885
AM	$D_{inte} = 0.10$ & $D_{load} = 0.05$	0.001	0.005	0.001
	$D_{inte} = 0.30$ & $D_{load} = 0.15$	0.001	0.006	0.004
	$D_{inte} = 0.50$ & $D_{load} = 0.25$	0.004	0.006	0.004
	$D_{inte} = 0.70$ & $D_{load} = 0.35$	0.003	0.005	0.003
	$D_{inte} = 0.90$ & $D_{load} = 0.45$	0.001	0.005	0.003

Note: D_{inte} = degree of noninvariant intercept; D_{load} = degree of noninvariant loading; N = sample size.

The change of Type I error rates when varying the noninvariance at the same indicator (i.e. two partially noninvariant conditions vs. one fully noninvariant condition) is compared. Figure 3.10 and Figure 3.11 compare the outcomes of testing intercepts and loadings respectively.

As shown in Figure 3.10, when testing the intercepts, the Type I error rates estimated by the AM method are not changed. However, the performances of the other two methods (i.e. the FR method and the B-H method) are impacted. Specifically, the Type I error rates estimated by the FR method are slightly reduced when compared to the partial noninvariant condition with a single noninvariant intercept. Yet, the Type I error rates are greatly increased when compared to the condition with a single noninvariant loading. For the B-H method, the fully noninvariant condition leads to the increase of the Type I error rates.

As shown in Figure 3.11, when testing the loadings, both the B-H method and the AM method behave similarly as the previous condition of testing the intercepts. After the indicator is modified to be fully noninvariant, the AM method is not affected at all, but the Type I errors estimated by the B-H method increase under most simulation conditions. For the FR method, the Type I error of testing loadings is not affected by the addition of noninvariant intercept onto the same indicator.

3.6.3.3 Power Rate

Table 3.17 and Table 3.18 report the power rates of testing the intercept when both measurement parameters (i.e. intercept and loading) at the first indicator are noninvariant.

Using the B-H method, no matter which parameter (i.e. the intercept or loading) is tested, the power rates increase as the sample size and noninvariance degree increase. With the AM method, the power rates of detecting the loading increase as the sample size and noninvariance degree increase, but the power rates of detecting the intercept only increase at the medium noninvariance degrees.

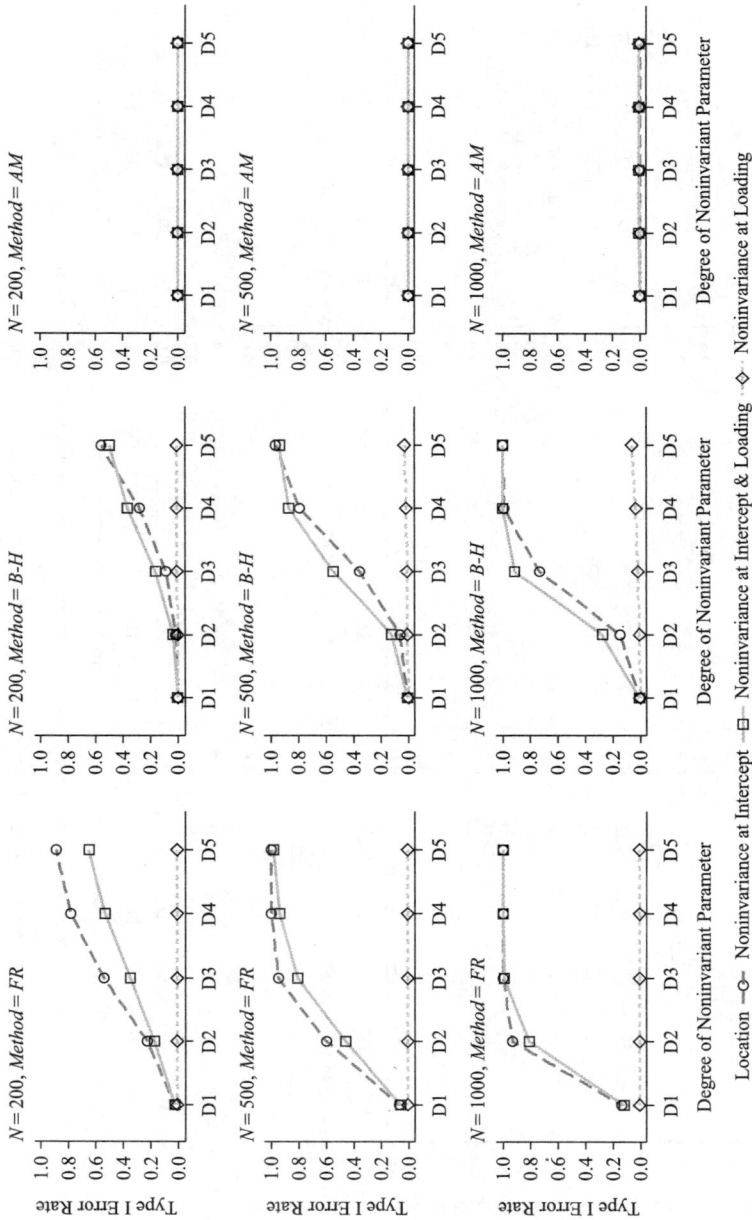

Figure 3.10　Type I error rates of testing intercepts with the variation of noninvariance at the same indicator

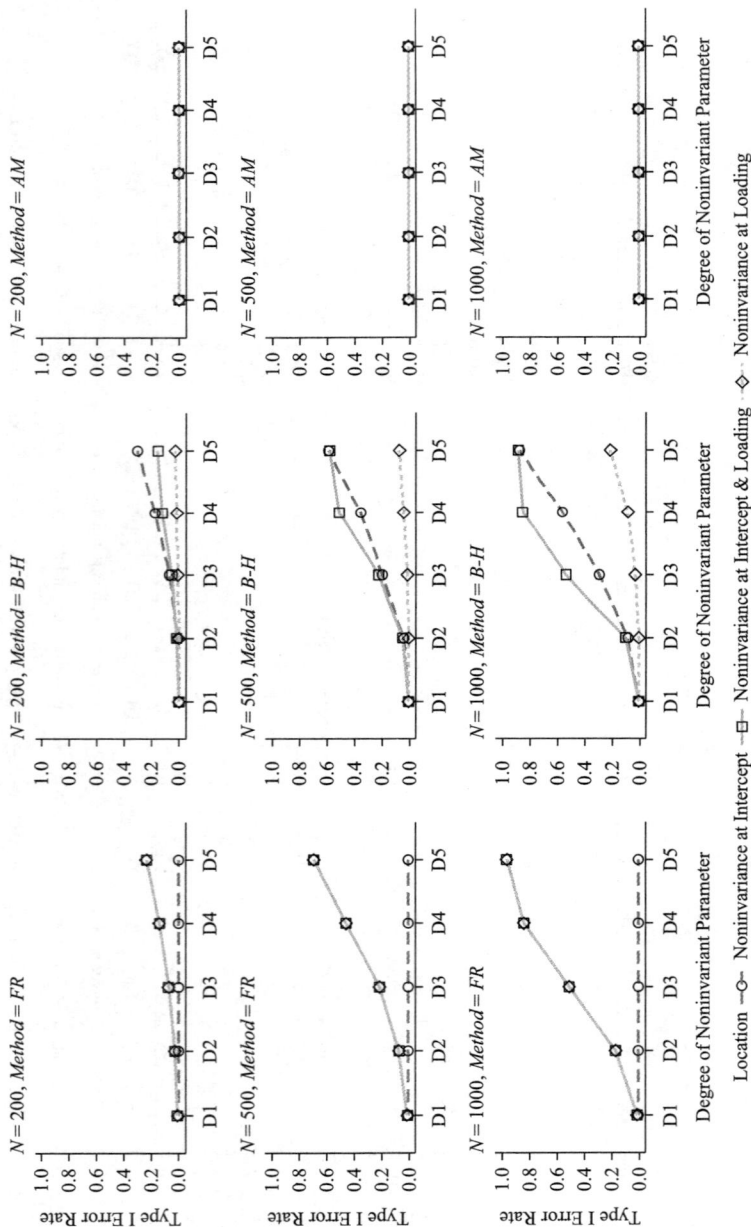

Figure 3.11 Type I error rates of testing loadings with the variation of noninvariance at the same indicator

Table 3.17　Power rates of testing intercepts with both noninvariant parameters at the same indicator

Method	D_{inte} & D_{load}	$N = 200$	$N = 500$	$N = 1000$
	$D_{inte} = 0.10$ & $D_{load} = 0.05$	0.025	0.090	0.240
	$D_{inte} = 0.30$ & $D_{load} = 0.15$	0.540	0.965	1.000
B-H	$D_{inte} = 0.50$ & $D_{load} = 0.25$	0.970	1.000	1.000
	$D_{inte} = 0.70$ & $D_{load} = 0.35$	1.000	1.000	1.000
	$D_{inte} = 0.90$ & $D_{load} = 0.45$	1.000	1.000	1.000
	$D_{inte} = 0.10$ & $D_{load} = 0.05$	0.010	0.025	0.070
	$D_{inte} = 0.30$ & $D_{load} = 0.15$	0.140	0.295	0.260
AM	$D_{inte} = 0.50$ & $D_{load} = 0.25$	0.290	0.285	0.165
	$D_{inte} = 0.70$ & $D_{load} = 0.35$	0.335	0.210	0.120
	$D_{inte} = 0.90$ & $D_{load} = 0.45$	0.280	0.170	0.100

Note: D_{inte} = degree of noninvariant intercept; D_{load} = degree of noninvariant loading; N = sample size.

Table 3.18　Power rates of testing loadings with both noninvariant parameters at the same indicator

Method	D_{inte} & D_{load}	$N = 200$	$N = 500$	$N = 1000$
	$D_{inte} = 0.10$ & $D_{load} = 0.05$	0.000	0.025	0.070
	$D_{inte} = 0.30$ & $D_{load} = 0.15$	0.260	0.725	0.970
B-H	$D_{inte} = 0.50$ & $D_{load} = 0.25$	0.735	0.995	1.000
	$D_{inte} = 0.70$ & $D_{load} = 0.35$	0.970	1.000	1.000
	$D_{inte} = 0.90$ & $D_{load} = 0.45$	1.000	1.000	1.000
	$D_{inte} = 0.10$ & $D_{load} = 0.05$	0.000	0.000	0.005
	$D_{inte} = 0.30$ & $D_{load} = 0.15$	0.005	0.035	0.190
AM	$D_{inte} = 0.50$ & $D_{load} = 0.25$	0.030	0.180	0.625
	$D_{inte} = 0.70$ & $D_{load} = 0.35$	0.075	0.495	0.930
	$D_{inte} = 0.90$ & $D_{load} = 0.45$	0.135	0.740	0.995

Note: D_{inte} = degree of noninvariant intercept; D_{load} = degree of noninvariant loading; N = sample size.

Figure 3.12 compares the power rates of detecting the intercept when varying the noninvariance at the same indicator. It is discovered that the B-H method is almost not affected when the indicator becomes fully noninvariant at both parameters. On the contrary, the power rates estimated by the AM method are reduced.

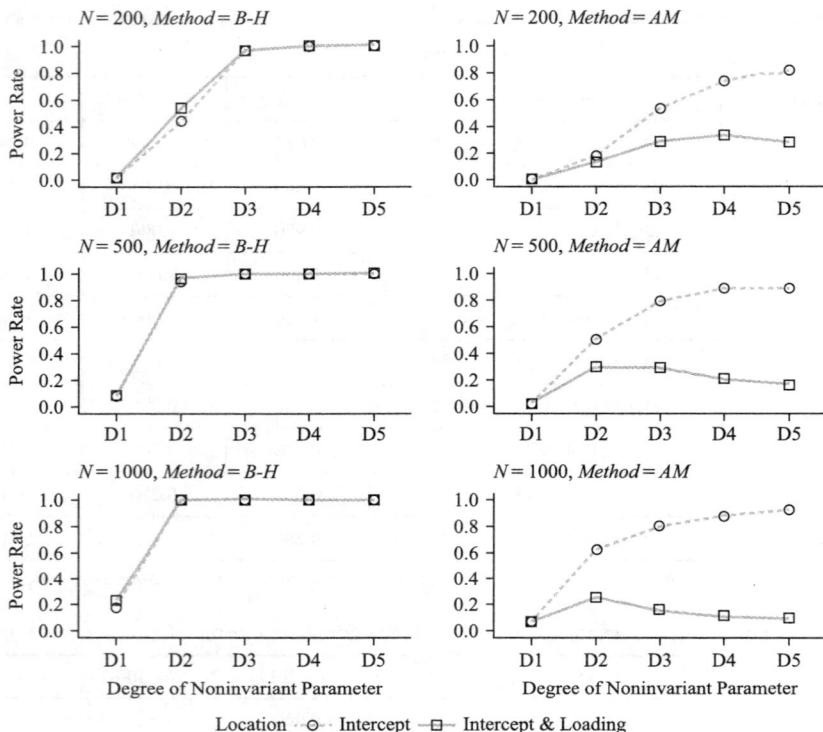

Figure 3.12　Power rates of testing intercepts with the variation of noninvariance at the same indicator

Figure 3.13 compares the power rates of detecting the loading when varying the noninvariance at the same indicator. Under the fully noninvariant condition, the power rates estimated by the B-H method are increased. In contrast, the power rates estimated by the AM method are not changed.

3.6.3.4　Design Effects

Table 3.19 presents the effect size (η^2) of design factors when varying the noninvariance at the same indicator. The results show that the testing method and the noninvariance degree have higher η^2 than the other factors and all the interaction terms. It suggests that these two main factors interpret more variance of the testing outcomes (i.e. the Type I error rate and power rate) than other factors.

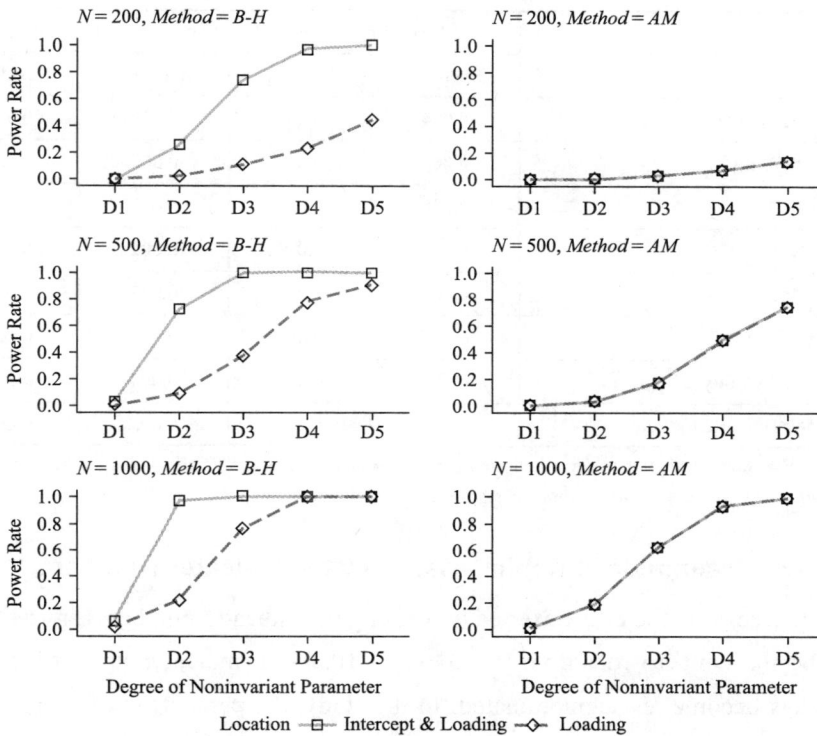

Figure 3.13 Power rates of testing loadings with the variation of noninvariance at the same indicator

Table 3.19 Effect size (η^2) of design factors with the variation of noninvariance at the same indicator

Design Factor	Type I Error Rate		Power Rate	
	Intercept	Loading	Intercept	Loading
Method	0.378	0.143	0.430	0.098
N	0.064	0.070	0.004	0.053
D	0.169	0.081	0.128	0.136
Partially/Fully	0.000	0.035	0.012	0.009
Method*N	0.032	0.041	0.003	0.027
Method*D	0.092	0.065	0.086	0.075
N*D	0.014	0.021	0.002	0.030

(to be continued)

Design Factor	Type I Error Rate		Power Rate	
	Intercept	Loading	Intercept	Loading
Method* Partially/Fully	0.004	0.049	0.029	0.014
N* Partially/Fully	0.001	0.017	0.002	0.003
D* Partially/Fully	0.038	0.054	0.011	0.005
Method*N*D	0.014	0.014	0.002	0.016
Method*N*Partially/Fully	0.001	0.013	0.002	0.005
Method*D* Partially/Fully	0.027	0.057	0.013	0.009
N*D* Partially/Fully	0.003	0.013	0.004	0.002
Method*N*D* Partially/Fully	0.008	0.011	0.003	0.003

Note: N = sample size; D = degree of noninvariant parameter; Partially/Fully = the condition for which one indicator was partially or fully noninvariant.

3.6.4 Magnitude of Noninvariance by the Indicator Number

In this section, the effect exerted by varying the indicator number is investigated. The indicator number varies from $P = 3$ to $P = 10$. As the indicator number increases, the models become less contaminated. In the study, the percentage of noninvariant parameters decreases from 17% (when $P = 3$) to 5% (when $P = 10$).

3.6.4.1 Perfect Recovery Rate

Table 3.20 reports the perfect recovery rates estimated by the B-H method when the magnitude of model noninvariance is simulated by varying the indicator number. It is observed that the perfect recovery rates are not consistently increased or decreased. The effect imposed by varying the indicator number is different depending on the type of noninvariant parameters. With the existence of noninvariant intercept, the increase of indicator number enhances the perfect recovery rates at the medium noninvariance degree (e.g. $D_{inte} = 0.50$ when $N = 200$; $D_{inte} = 0.30$ when $N = 500$ or 1000), but is not so when the noninvariance degree is larger or smaller. With the existence of noninvariant loading, the increase of indicator number enhances the perfect recovery rates at large noninvariance degrees (e.g. $D_{load} \geqslant 0.25$ when $N = 200$; $D_{load} \geqslant 0.15$ when $N = 500$ or 1000).

Table 3.20   Perfect recovery rates with the B-H method when varying the indicator number

P	D_{inte}	Noninvariant intercepts			D_{load}	Noninvariant loadings		
		$N = 200$	$N = 500$	$N = 1000$		$N = 200$	$N = 500$	$N = 1000$
$P = 3$		0.000	0.055	0.060		0.010	0.000	0.025
$P = 5$	$D_{inte} = 0.10$	0.020	0.050	0.170	$D_{load} = 0.05$	0.000	0.000	0.015
$P = 7$		0.005	0.015	0.140		0.005	0.005	0.020
$P = 10$		0.005	0.045	0.160		0.015	0.000	0.010
$P = 3$		0.150	0.235	0.110		0.010	0.035	0.085
$P = 5$	$D_{inte} = 0.30$	0.340	0.620	0.395	$D_{load} = 0.15$	0.025	0.070	0.205
$P = 7$		0.350	0.750	0.530		0.000	0.100	0.330
$P = 10$		0.340	0.855	0.780		0.050	0.140	0.415
$P = 3$		0.270	0.130	0.005		0.040	0.065	0.210
$P = 5$	$D_{inte} = 0.50$	0.515	0.070	0.000	$D_{load} = 0.25$	0.090	0.280	0.615
$P = 7$		0.680	0.305	0.030		0.090	0.520	0.765
$P = 10$		0.810	0.565	0.185		0.175	0.565	0.855
$P = 3$		0.265	0.055	0.000		0.050	0.130	0.320
$P = 5$	$D_{inte} = 0.70$	0.170	0.000	0.000	$D_{load} = 0.35$	0.190	0.570	0.635
$P = 7$		0.355	0.020	0.000		0.260	0.805	0.650
$P = 10$		0.580	0.130	0.000		0.430	0.850	0.770
$P = 3$		0.265	0.030	0.000		0.080	0.225	0.465
$P = 5$	$D_{inte} = 0.90$	0.005	0.000	0.000	$D_{load} = 0.45$	0.325	0.585	0.310
$P = 7$		0.080	0.000	0.000		0.505	0.765	0.390
$P = 10$		0.265	0.000	0.000		0.665	0.785	0.560

Note: P = number of indicators; D_{inte} = degree of noninvariant intercept; D_{load} = degree of noninvariant loading; N = sample size.

Table 3.21 reports the perfect recovery rates estimated by the AM method when varying the indicator number. As shown in this table, the perfect recovery rate increases with the increase of the indicator number at large noninvariance degrees (e.g. $D_{inte} \geqslant 0.30$ or $D_{load} \geqslant 0.15$). This tendency remains the same no matter whether the noninvariance is located at the intercept or loading.

Table 3.21　Perfect recovery rates with the AM method when varying the indicator number

P	D_{inte}	Noninvariant intercepts			D_{load}	Noninvariant loadings		
		$N = 200$	$N = 500$	$N = 1000$		$N = 200$	$N = 500$	$N = 1000$
$P = 3$		0.010	0.005	0.010		0.005	0.000	0.005
$P = 5$	$D_{\text{inte}} = 0.10$	0.005	0.020	0.070	$D_{\text{load}} = 0.05$	0.000	0.000	0.005
$P = 7$		0.005	0.030	0.100		0.005	0.010	0.025
$P = 10$		0.005	0.045	0.165		0.005	0.010	0.025
$P = 3$		0.110	0.210	0.290		0.000	0.000	0.025
$P = 5$	$D_{\text{inte}} = 0.30$	0.180	0.500	0.630	$D_{\text{load}} = 0.15$	0.005	0.035	0.190
$P = 7$		0.295	0.685	0.790		0.005	0.080	0.340
$P = 10$		0.345	0.760	0.890		0.035	0.170	0.555
$P = 3$		0.225	0.385	0.400		0.000	0.010	0.110
$P = 5$	$D_{\text{inte}} = 0.50$	0.525	0.780	0.810	$D_{\text{load}} = 0.25$	0.030	0.180	0.625
$P = 7$		0.695	0.875	0.905		0.050	0.475	0.890
$P = 10$		0.760	0.900	0.955		0.130	0.590	0.930
$P = 3$		0.360	0.420	0.455		0.005	0.050	0.250
$P = 5$	$D_{\text{inte}} = 0.70$	0.735	0.870	0.880	$D_{\text{load}} = 0.35$	0.075	0.490	0.910
$P = 7$		0.830	0.925	0.925		0.155	0.795	0.965
$P = 10$		0.895	0.920	0.965		0.340	0.895	0.945
$P = 3$		0.380	0.490	0.525		0.005	0.115	0.430
$P = 5$	$D_{\text{inte}} = 0.90$	0.810	0.875	0.925	$D_{\text{load}} = 0.45$	0.135	0.725	0.975
$P = 7$		0.875	0.950	0.935		0.335	0.930	0.960
$P = 10$		0.920	0.925	0.970		0.580	0.930	0.940

Note: P = number of indicators; D_{inte} = degree of noninvariant intercept; D_{load} = degree of noninvariant loading; N = sample size.

The effect of indicator number on perfect recovery rate is compared between the B-H method and the AM method. As shown in Figure 3.14, with the existence of noninvariant intercept, the AM method performs better than the B-H method at large noninvariance degrees. The AM method retrieves higher perfect recovery rates at $D_{\text{inte}} \geqslant 0.70$ when $N = 200$, and at $D_{\text{inte}} \geqslant 0.50$ when $N = 500$ or 1000.

As shown in Figure 3.15, with the existence of noninvariant loading, both the B-H method and the AM method perform similarly under the majority of simulation

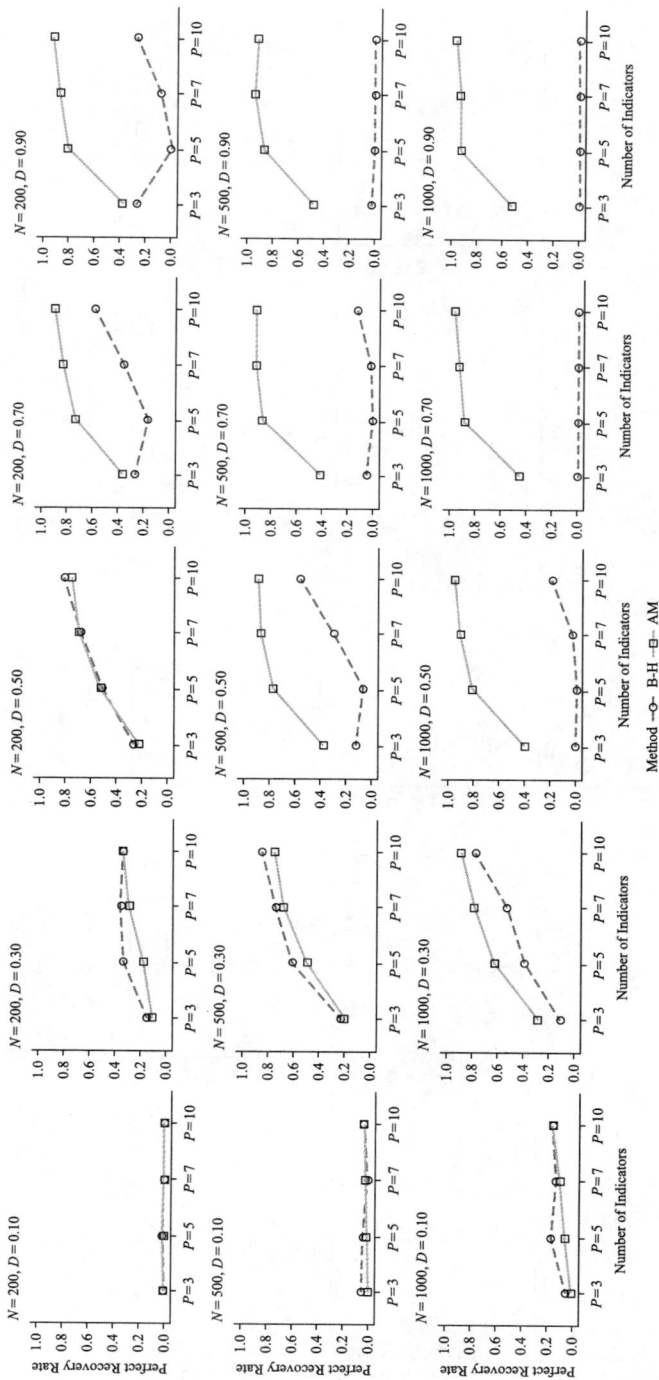

Figure 3.14   Perfect recovery rates for models with noninvariance in the intercept when varying the indicator number

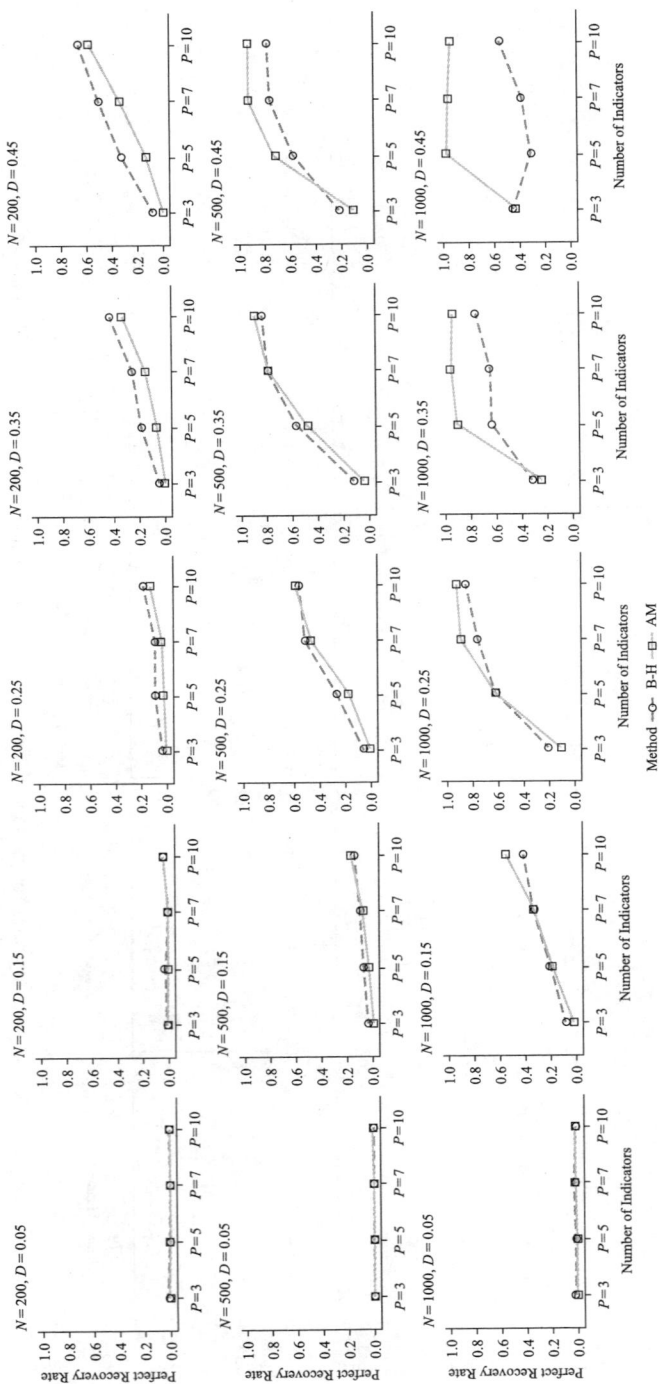

Figure 3.15　Perfect recovery rates for models with noninvariance in the loadings when varying the indicator number

conditions. Only under some extreme conditions (e.g. $D_{\text{load}} \geqslant 0.35$, $P \geqslant 5$ and $N = 1000$), the AM method performs greatly better than the B-H method.

3.6.4.2   Type I Error Rate

In Table 3.22 and Table 3.23, the Type I error rates of testing invariant intercepts and loading by the FR method are summarized respectively. In general, the increase of indicator number leads to the increase of the Type I errors under the following two conditions: 1) the testing of intercepts when models are contaminated by noninvariant intercept; 2) the testing of loadings when models are contaminated by noninvariant loading. This effect of indicator number on the Type I error rate is clearly manifested when the noninvariance degree is large (e.g. $D_{\text{inte}} \geqslant 0.50$ when testing intercepts and $D_{\text{load}} \geqslant 0.25$ when testing loadings).

Table 3.22   Type I error rates of testing intercepts by the FR method when varying the indicator number

P	D_{inte}	Noninvariant intercepts			D_{load}	Noninvariant loadings		
		$N = 200$	$N = 500$	$N = 1000$		$N = 200$	$N = 500$	$N = 1000$
$P = 3$		0.028	0.093	0.133		0.013	0.013	0.015
$P = 5$	$D_{\text{inte}} = 0.10$	0.029	0.064	0.133	$D_{\text{load}} = 0.05$	0.008	0.006	0.006
$P = 7$		0.010	0.036	0.104		0.003	0.003	0.004
$P = 10$		0.012	0.031	0.080		0.001	0.002	0.002
$P = 3$		0.193	0.520	0.838		0.015	0.013	0.013
$P = 5$	$D_{\text{inte}} = 0.30$	0.228	0.601	0.929	$D_{\text{load}} = 0.15$	0.009	0.005	0.006
$P = 7$		0.190	0.586	0.938		0.003	0.003	0.004
$P = 10$		0.153	0.598	0.926		0.001	0.003	0.003
$P = 3$		0.415	0.843	1.000		0.015	0.013	0.010
$P = 5$	$D_{\text{inte}} = 0.50$	0.540	0.949	1.000	$D_{\text{load}} = 0.25$	0.010	0.004	0.005
$P = 7$		0.523	0.959	1.000		0.003	0.003	0.003
$P = 10$		0.522	0.968	1.000		0.002	0.003	0.002
$P = 3$		0.545	0.953	1.000		0.015	0.010	0.015
$P = 5$	$D_{\text{inte}} = 0.70$	0.784	0.998	1.000	$D_{\text{load}} = 0.35$	0.009	0.005	0.005
$P = 7$		0.773	0.997	1.000		0.004	0.003	0.003
$P = 10$		0.807	0.999	1.000		0.002	0.003	0.002

(to be continued)

P	D_{inte}	Noninvariant intercepts			D_{load}	Noninvariant loadings		
		$N = 200$	$N = 500$	$N = 1000$		$N = 200$	$N = 500$	$N = 1000$
$P = 3$	$D_{\text{inte}} = 0.90$	0.625	0.985	1.000	$D_{\text{load}} = 0.45$	0.015	0.005	0.018
$P = 5$		0.893	1.000	1.000		0.008	0.005	0.006
$P = 7$		0.890	1.000	1.000		0.003	0.003	0.002
$P = 10$		0.918	1.000	1.000		0.002	0.003	0.002

Note: P = number of indicators; D_{inte} = degree of noninvariant intercept; D_{load} = degree of noninvariant loading; N = sample size.

However, under the other two conditions (i.e. testing invariant intercepts while noninvariance is located at the loading; testing invariant loading while the noninvariance is located at the intercept), the Type I error rate is slightly reduced as the indicator number increases.

Table 3.23　Type I error rates of testing loadings by the FR method when varying the indicator number

P	D_{inte}	Noninvariant intercepts			D_{load}	Noninvariant loadings		
		$N = 200$	$N = 500$	$N = 1000$		$N = 200$	$N = 500$	$N = 1000$
$P = 3$	$D_{\text{inte}} = 0.10$	0.020	0.018	0.008	$D_{\text{load}} = 0.05$	0.028	0.015	0.018
$P = 5$		0.003	0.008	0.003		0.005	0.011	0.015
$P = 7$		0.006	0.003	0.003		0.007	0.014	0.018
$P = 10$		0.008	0.002	0.001		0.012	0.005	0.011
$P = 3$	$D_{\text{inte}} = 0.30$	0.020	0.018	0.008	$D_{\text{load}} = 0.15$	0.043	0.055	0.123
$P = 5$		0.003	0.008	0.003		0.024	0.073	0.170
$P = 7$		0.006	0.003	0.003		0.021	0.077	0.220
$P = 10$		0.008	0.002	0.001		0.041	0.074	0.192
$P = 3$	$D_{\text{inte}} = 0.50$	0.020	0.018	0.008	$D_{\text{load}} = 0.25$	0.075	0.135	0.315
$P = 5$		0.003	0.008	0.003		0.074	0.214	0.514
$P = 7$		0.006	0.003	0.003		0.070	0.273	0.605
$P = 10$		0.008	0.002	0.001		0.089	0.282	0.659

(to be continued)

P	D_{inte}	Noninvariant intercepts			D_{load}	Noninvariant loadings		
		$N = 200$	$N = 500$	$N = 1000$		$N = 200$	$N = 500$	$N = 1000$
$P = 3$		0.020	0.018	0.008		0.118	0.248	0.558
$P = 5$	$D_{\text{inte}} = 0.70$	0.003	0.008	0.003	$D_{\text{load}} = 0.35$	0.143	0.461	0.841
$P = 7$		0.006	0.003	0.003		0.164	0.568	0.913
$P = 10$		0.008	0.002	0.001		0.171	0.567	0.938
$P = 3$		0.020	0.018	0.008		0.155	0.388	0.768
$P = 5$	$D_{\text{inte}} = 0.90$	0.003	0.008	0.003	$D_{\text{load}} = 0.45$	0.239	0.698	0.969
$P = 7$		0.006	0.003	0.003		0.277	0.795	0.984
$P = 10$		0.008	0.002	0.001		0.294	0.819	0.996

Note: P = number of indicators; D_{inte} = degree of noninvariant intercept; D_{load} = degree of noninvariant loading; N = sample size.

Table 3.24 and Table 3.25 report the Type I error rates estimated by the B-H method in testing invariant intercepts and loadings respectively. Generally speaking, no matter which type of parameter is tested, large indicator number is able to mitigate the Type I errors. Only at large noninvariance degrees (e.g. $D_{\text{inte}} \geqslant 0.70$, or $D_{\text{load}} \geqslant 0.35$), can the Type I error rates be increased when the indicator number changes from $P = 3$ to $P = 5$.

Table 3.24　Type I error rates of testing intercepts by the B-H method when varying the indicator numbers

P	D_{inte}	Noninvariant intercepts			D_{load}	Noninvariant loadings		
		$N = 200$	$N = 500$	$N = 1000$		$N = 200$	$N = 500$	$N = 1000$
$P = 3$		0.010	0.013	0.048		0.005	0.000	0.007
$P = 5$	$D_{\text{inte}} = 0.10$	0.004	0.006	0.004	$D_{\text{load}} = 0.05$	0.004	0.002	0.000
$P = 7$		0.006	0.001	0.003		0.004	0.000	0.001
$P = 10$		0.000	0.002	0.001		0.000	0.001	0.000
$P = 3$		0.055	0.228	0.558		0.008	0.002	0.015
$P = 5$	$D_{\text{inte}} = 0.30$	0.021	0.055	0.143	$D_{\text{load}} = 0.15$	0.003	0.005	0.001
$P = 7$		0.011	0.018	0.046		0.004	0.001	0.004
$P = 10$		0.002	0.006	0.010		0.000	0.002	0.002

(to be continued)

P	D_{inte}	Noninvariant intercepts			D_{load}	Noninvariant loadings		
		$N = 200$	$N = 500$	$N = 1000$		$N = 200$	$N = 500$	$N = 1000$
$P = 3$		0.150	0.493	0.853		0.008	0.007	0.027
$P = 5$		0.090	0.353	0.730		0.005	0.010	0.011
$P = 7$	$D_{\text{inte}} = 0.50$	0.023	0.088	0.256	$D_{\text{load}} = 0.25$	0.006	0.001	0.009
$P = 10$		0.005	0.016	0.048		0.001	0.004	0.005
$P = 3$		0.205	0.518	0.843		0.008	0.015	0.043
$P = 5$		0.283	0.793	0.994		0.009	0.017	0.027
$P = 7$	$D_{\text{inte}} = 0.70$	0.058	0.289	0.718	$D_{\text{load}} = 0.35$	0.007	0.003	0.024
$P = 10$		0.013	0.057	0.184		0.001	0.007	0.014
$P = 3$		0.170	0.425	0.775		0.010	0.020	0.052
$P = 5$		0.555	0.970	1.000		0.009	0.028	0.055
$P = 7$	$D_{\text{inte}} = 0.90$	0.191	0.643	0.951	$D_{\text{load}} = 0.45$	0.010	0.011	0.047
$P = 10$		0.031	0.131	0.440		0.001	0.014	0.028

Note: P = number of indicators; D_{inte} = degree of noninvariant intercept; D_{load} = degree of noninvariant loading; N = sample size.

Table 3.25　Type I error rates of testing loadings by the B-H method when varying the indicator numbers

P	D_{inte}	Noninvariant intercepts			D_{load}	Noninvariant loadings		
		$N = 200$	$N = 500$	$N = 1000$		$N = 200$	$N = 500$	$N = 1000$
$P = 3$		0.015	0.010	0.022		0.013	0.010	0.003
$P = 5$		0.001	0.006	0.004		0.001	0.004	0.001
$P = 7$	$D_{\text{inte}} = 0.10$	0.003	0.002	0.003	$D_{\text{load}} = 0.05$	0.003	0.003	0.000
$P = 10$		0.002	0.001	0.001		0.001	0.001	0.000
$P = 3$		0.043	0.118	0.317		0.018	0.008	0.018
$P = 5$		0.012	0.039	0.079		0.001	0.008	0.006
$P = 7$	$D_{\text{inte}} = 0.30$	0.006	0.016	0.049	$D_{\text{load}} = 0.15$	0.005	0.003	0.004
$P = 10$		0.004	0.008	0.016		0.001	0.001	0.002

(to be continued)

P	D_{inte}	Noninvariant intercepts			D_{load}	Noninvariant loadings		
		$N = 200$	$N = 500$	$N = 1000$		$N = 200$	$N = 500$	$N = 1000$
$P = 3$		0.132	0.337	0.552		0.020	0.020	0.060
$P = 5$	$D_{inte} = 0.50$	0.070	0.200	0.293	$D_{load} = 0.25$	0.008	0.016	0.034
$P = 7$		0.037	0.088	0.151		0.007	0.007	0.019
$P = 10$		0.014	0.038	0.077		0.001	0.003	0.005
$P = 3$		0.208	0.402	0.550		0.020	0.043	0.105
$P = 5$	$D_{inte} = 0.70$	0.175	0.357	0.567	$D_{load} = 0.35$	0.014	0.041	0.081
$P = 7$		0.086	0.161	0.224		0.015	0.015	0.051
$P = 10$		0.038	0.086	0.109		0.003	0.008	0.012
$P = 3$		0.242	0.395	0.503		0.025	0.058	0.143
$P = 5$	$D_{inte} = 0.90$	0.302	0.594	0.878	$D_{load} = 0.45$	0.024	0.073	0.210
$P = 7$		0.141	0.224	0.354		0.018	0.038	0.124
$P = 10$		0.069	0.110	0.127		0.006	0.014	0.031

Note: P = number of indicators; D_{inte} = degree of noninvariant intercept; D_{load} = degree of noninvariant loading; N = sample size.

In Table 3.26 and Table 3.27, the Type I error rates of testing invariant intercepts/ loading by the AM method are reported respectively. As shown in these two tables, when choosing the AM method, the change of indicator numbers does not affect the results. The Type I errors are zeroes or close to zeroes under all simulation conditions.

Table 3.26   Type I error rates of testing intercepts by the AM method when varying the indicator number

P	D_{inte}	Noninvariant intercepts			D_{load}	Noninvariant loadings		
		$N = 200$	$N = 500$	$N = 1000$		$N = 200$	$N = 500$	$N = 1000$
$P = 3$		0.000	0.000	0.000		0.000	0.000	0.002
$P = 5$	$D_{inte} = 0.10$	0.001	0.000	0.000	$D_{load} = 0.05$	0.001	0.000	0.000
$P = 7$		0.000	0.000	0.001		0.001	0.000	0.003
$P = 10$		0.000	0.001	0.002		0.001	0.002	0.002

(*to be continued*)

P	D_{inte}	Noninvariant intercepts			D_{load}	Noninvariant loadings		
		$N = 200$	$N = 500$	$N = 1000$		$N = 200$	$N = 500$	$N = 1000$
$P = 3$		0.000	0.000	0.003		0.000	0.000	0.002
$P = 5$	$D_{inte} = 0.30$	0.000	0.000	0.000	$D_{load} = 0.15$	0.003	0.000	0.000
$P = 7$		0.000	0.000	0.001		0.001	0.001	0.002
$P = 10$		0.000	0.001	0.002		0.001	0.002	0.003
$P = 3$		0.000	0.000	0.003		0.000	0.000	0.003
$P = 5$	$D_{inte} = 0.50$	0.000	0.000	0.000	$D_{load} = 0.25$	0.003	0.000	0.001
$P = 7$		0.000	0.000	0.001		0.001	0.001	0.001
$P = 10$		0.000	0.001	0.002		0.001	0.002	0.004
$P = 3$		0.000	0.000	0.000		0.002	0.000	0.003
$P = 5$	$D_{inte} = 0.70$	0.000	0.000	0.000	$D_{load} = 0.35$	0.002	0.001	0.002
$P = 7$		0.001	0.000	0.002		0.001	0.001	0.002
$P = 10$		0.000	0.001	0.002		0.001	0.003	0.004
$P = 3$		0.000	0.000	0.000		0.002	0.000	0.005
$P = 5$	$D_{inte} = 0.90$	0.000	0.000	0.000	$D_{load} = 0.45$	0.003	0.001	0.002
$P = 7$		0.001	0.000	0.002		0.001	0.001	0.002
$P = 10$		0.000	0.001	0.001		0.001	0.003	0.005

Note: P = number of indicators; D_{inte} = degree of noninvariant intercept; D_{load} = degree of noninvariant loading; N = sample size.

The effect of indicator number on the Type I error rate is compared among the three methods. Figure 3.16 and Figure 3.17 compare the outcomes of testing invariant intercepts when the noninvariance is located at intercept/loading respectively. With noninvariant intercept in the models (see Figure 3.16), both the FR method and the AM method are not largely affected by the change of indicator number. Yet, for the B-H method, the Type I error rates is reduced as the indicator number increased. With noninvariant loading in the models (see Figure 3.17), all the three methods are not largely impacted by the change of indicator number.

Figure 3.18 and Figure 3.19 compare the outcomes of testing invariant loadings when the noninvariance is located at intercept/loading respectively. With the existence of noninvariant intercept (see Figure 3.18), both the FR and the AM methods are not

Table 3.27　Type I error rates of testing loadings by the AM method when varying the indicator number

P	D_{inte}	Noninvariant intercepts			D_{load}	Noninvariant loadings		
		$N = 200$	$N = 500$	$N = 1000$		$N = 200$	$N = 500$	$N = 1000$
$P = 3$		0.003	0.002	0.000		0.003	0.003	0.000
$P = 5$	$D_{inte} = 0.10$	0.001	0.005	0.001	$D_{load} = 0.05$	0.001	0.005	0.001
$P = 7$		0.008	0.005	0.004		0.008	0.004	0.004
$P = 10$		0.005	0.006	0.003		0.004	0.005	0.003
$P = 3$		0.003	0.002	0.000		0.003	0.005	0.003
$P = 5$	$D_{inte} = 0.30$	0.001	0.005	0.001	$D_{load} = 0.15$	0.001	0.006	0.004
$P = 7$		0.008	0.005	0.004		0.008	0.004	0.006
$P = 10$		0.005	0.006	0.003		0.004	0.006	0.003
$P = 3$		0.003	0.002	0.000		0.005	0.008	0.003
$P = 5$	$D_{inte} = 0.50$	0.001	0.005	0.001	$D_{load} = 0.25$	0.004	0.006	0.004
$P = 7$		0.008	0.005	0.004		0.008	0.005	0.005
$P = 10$		0.005	0.006	0.003		0.004	0.004	0.003
$P = 3$		0.003	0.002	0.000		0.005	0.015	0.008
$P = 5$	$D_{inte} = 0.70$	0.001	0.005	0.001	$D_{load} = 0.35$	0.003	0.005	0.003
$P = 7$		0.008	0.005	0.004		0.008	0.004	0.003
$P = 10$		0.005	0.006	0.003		0.004	0.004	0.002
$P = 3$		0.003	0.002	0.000		0.005	0.010	0.015
$P = 5$	$D_{inte} = 0.90$	0.001	0.005	0.001	$D_{load} = 0.45$	0.001	0.005	0.003
$P = 7$		0.008	0.005	0.004		0.009	0.003	0.004
$P = 10$		0.005	0.006	0.003		0.004	0.004	0.003

Note: P = number of indicators; D_{inte} = degree of noninvariant intercept; D_{load} = degree of noninvariant loading; N = sample size.

affected. The Type I error rate is kept at low levels under all simulation conditions. However, for the B-H method, the Type I error rates is reduced as the indicator number increases. With noninvariant loading in the models (see Figure 3.19), both the B-H and the AM methods are not largely affected. Yet, the Type I errors given by the FR method become severe as the indicator number increases.

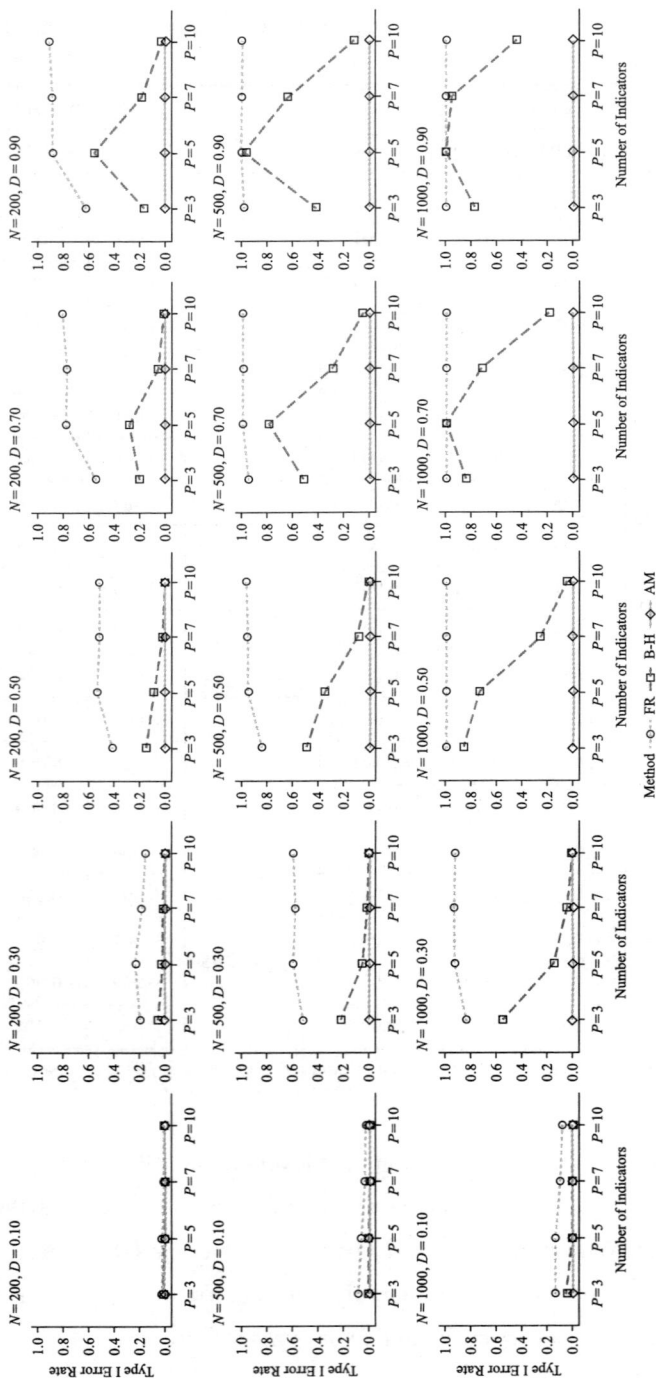

Figure 3.16　Type I error rates of testing intercepts for models with noninvariance in the intercept when varying the indicator number

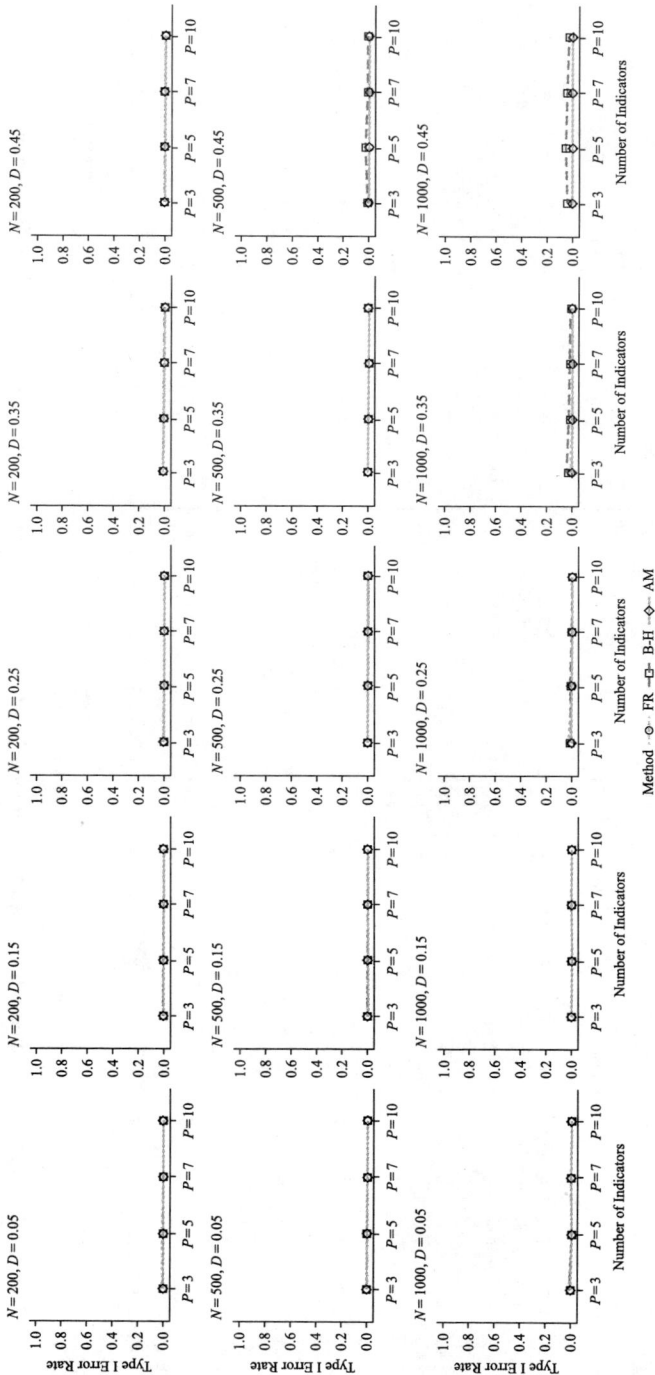

Figure 3.17　Type I error rates of testing intercepts for models with noninvariance in the loading when varying the indicator number

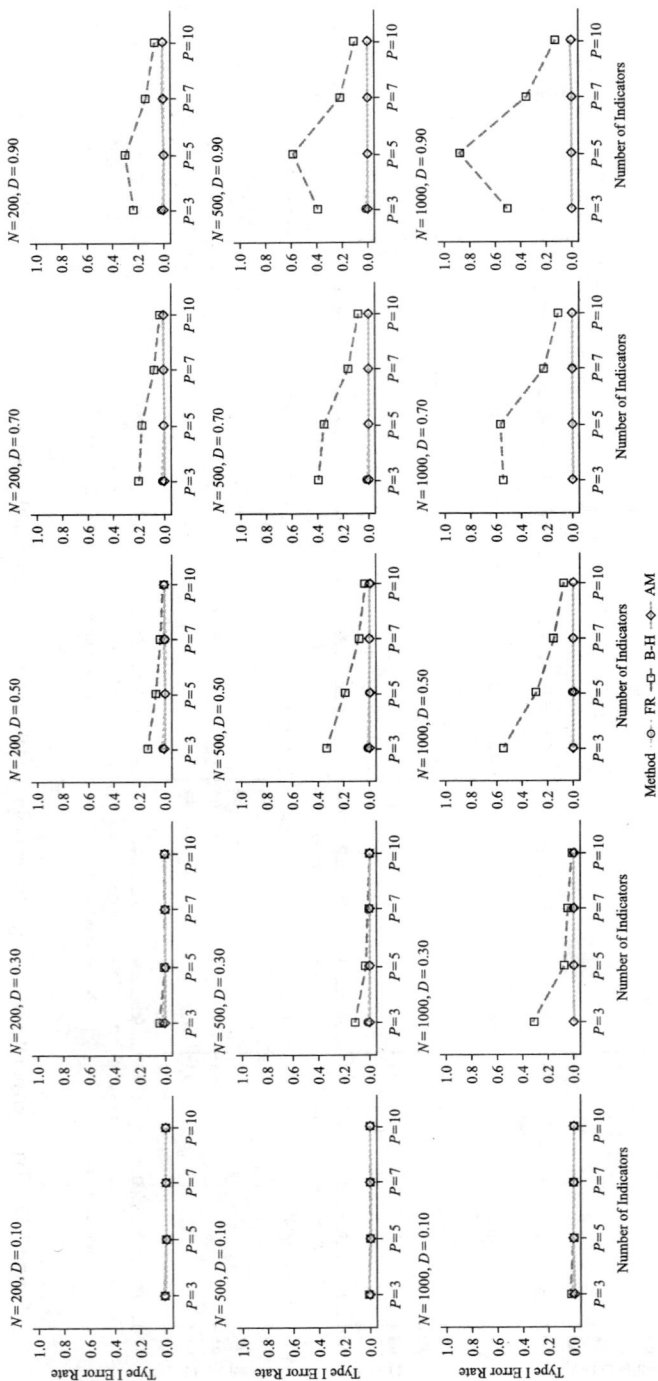

Figure 3.18　Type I error rates of testing loadings for models with noninvariance in the intercept when varying the indicator number

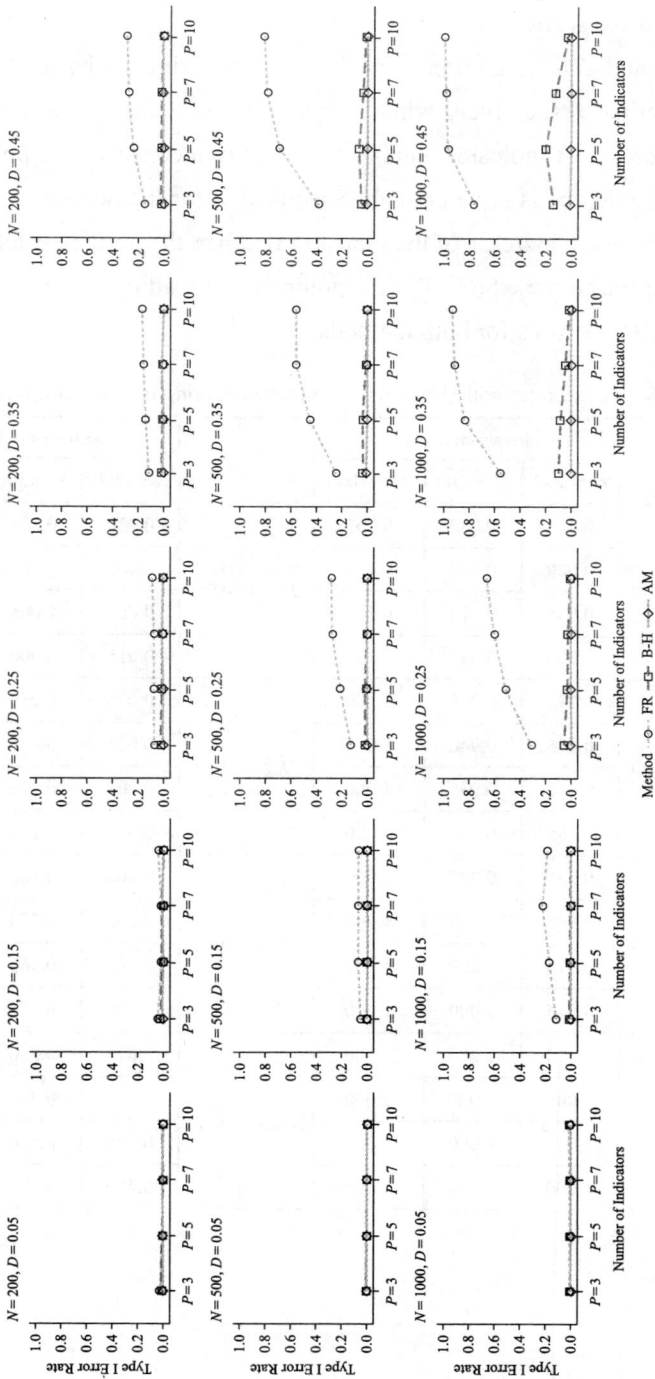

Figure 3.19　Type I error rates of testing loadings for models with noninvariance in the loading when varying the indicator number

3.6.4.3 Power Rate

Table 3.28 and Table 3.29 report the power rates estimated by the B-H method and the AM method respectively when varying the indicator number. Using both methods, the increase of indicator number leads to the increase of the power rates if the noninvariance degree is large enough. Specifically, for the noninvariant intercept at $D_{\text{inte}} \geqslant 0.30$, with the increase of the indicator number, the positive effect on power rates is observed for both methods. For the noninvariant loading, the positive effect is observed when $D_{\text{load}} \geqslant 0.15$ for both methods.

Table 3.28　Power rates with the B-H method when varying the indicator number

P	D_{inte}	Noninvariant intercepts			D_{load}	Noninvariant loadings		
		$N = 200$	$N = 500$	$N = 1000$		$N = 200$	$N = 500$	$N = 1000$
$P = 3$		0.010	0.080	0.165		0.020	0.005	0.025
$P = 5$	$D_{\text{inte}} = 0.10$	0.020	0.080	0.185	$D_{\text{load}} = 0.05$	0.000	0.000	0.015
$P = 7$		0.005	0.020	0.165		0.005	0.005	0.020
$P = 10$		0.005	0.045	0.165		0.015	0.000	0.010
$P = 3$		0.295	0.700	0.980		0.025	0.050	0.125
$P = 5$	$D_{\text{inte}} = 0.30$	0.445	0.940	1.000	$D_{\text{load}} = 0.15$	0.025	0.085	0.225
$P = 7$		0.410	0.935	1.000		0.005	0.115	0.360
$P = 10$		0.385	0.960	1.000		0.050	0.150	0.435
$P = 3$		0.655	0.985	1.000		0.060	0.105	0.335
$P = 5$	$D_{\text{inte}} = 0.50$	0.965	1.000	1.000	$D_{\text{load}} = 0.25$	0.105	0.370	0.775
$P = 7$		0.975	1.000	1.000		0.125	0.560	0.920
$P = 10$		0.975	1.000	1.000		0.180	0.610	0.945
$P = 3$		0.820	1.000	1.000		0.075	0.220	0.555
$P = 5$	$D_{\text{inte}} = 0.70$	1.000	1.000	1.000	$D_{\text{load}} = 0.35$	0.240	0.775	0.990
$P = 7$		1.000	1.000	1.000		0.345	0.890	1.000
$P = 10$		1.000	1.000	1.000		0.450	0.975	1.000

(to be continued)

P	D_{inte}	Noninvariant intercepts			D_{load}	Noninvariant loadings		
		N = 200	N = 500	N = 1000		N = 200	N = 500	N = 1000
P = 3		0.900	1.000	1.000		0.115	0.345	0.800
P = 5	D_{inte} = 0.90	1.000	1.000	1.000	D_{load} = 0.45	0.450	0.910	1.000
P = 7		1.000	1.000	1.000		0.640	0.995	1.000
P = 10		1.000	1.000	1.000		0.715	1.000	1.000

Note: P = number of indicators; D_{inte} = degree of noninvariant intercept; D_{load} = degree of noninvariant loading; N = sample size.

Table 3.29 Power rates with the AM method when varying the indicator number

P	D_{inte}	Noninvariant intercepts			D_{load}	Noninvariant loadings		
		N = 200	N = 500	N = 1000		N = 200	N = 500	N = 1000
P = 3		0.010	0.005	0.010		0.005	0.000	0.005
P = 5	D_{inte} = 0.10	0.005	0.020	0.070	D_{load} = 0.05	0.000	0.000	0.005
P = 7		0.005	0.035	0.100		0.005	0.010	0.025
P = 10		0.005	0.050	0.170		0.010	0.010	0.025
P = 3		0.110	0.210	0.290		0.000	0.000	0.025
P = 5	D_{inte} = 0.30	0.185	0.510	0.630	D_{load} = 0.15	0.005	0.035	0.190
P = 7		0.300	0.720	0.815		0.005	0.085	0.350
P = 10		0.360	0.820	0.925		0.040	0.175	0.570
P = 3		0.225	0.390	0.400		0.000	0.010	0.110
P = 5	D_{inte} = 0.50	0.530	0.790	0.810	D_{load} = 0.25	0.030	0.180	0.625
P = 7		0.740	0.910	0.930		0.050	0.495	0.930
P = 10		0.790	0.960	0.990		0.145	0.620	0.990
P = 3		0.365	0.425	0.455		0.005	0.050	0.260
P = 5	D_{inte} = 0.70	0.740	0.885	0.880	D_{load} = 0.35	0.075	0.495	0.930
P = 7		0.885	0.960	0.960		0.160	0.815	1.000
P = 10		0.925	0.980	1.000		0.360	0.945	1.000

(to be continued)

P	D_{inte}	Noninvariant intercepts			D_{load}	Noninvariant loadings		
		$N = 200$	$N = 500$	$N = 1000$		$N = 200$	$N = 500$	$N = 1000$
$P = 3$		0.385	0.495	0.525		0.005	0.120	0.450
$P = 5$	$D_{\text{inte}} = 0.90$	0.815	0.890	0.930	$D_{\text{load}} = 0.45$	0.135	0.740	0.995
$P = 7$		0.935	0.985	0.970		0.345	0.955	1.000
$P = 10$		0.955	0.985	1.000		0.610	0.995	1.000

Note: P = number of indicators; D_{inte} = degree of noninvariant intercept; D_{load} = degree of noninvariant loading; N = sample size.

In Figure 3.20, the B-H method and the AM method are compared on the recovery of truly noninvariant intercept when varying the indicator number. At the smallest noninvariance degree (i.e. $D_{\text{inte}} = 0.10$), both methods are almost not impacted by the change of indicator number. However, when the noninvariance degree is large (i.e. $D_{\text{inte}} > 0.10$), the increase of indicator numbers leads to the increased power rates for both methods. The AM method is affected more seriously by the increase of the indicator number than the B-H method.

In Figure 3.21, the B-H method and the AM method are compared on the detection of truly noninvariant loading when varying the indicator numbers. It is discovered that both methods are not largely affected if the noninvariant degree of the loading parameter is small (e.g. $D_{\text{load}} \leqslant 0.15$ when $N = 200$ or 500, and $D_{\text{load}} = 0.05$ when $N = 1000$). When the noninvariance degree becomes large, the power rates estimated by both methods increase.

3.6.4.4　Design Effects

Table 3.30 presents the effect sizes (η^2) of the main factors and interaction terms when varying the indicator number. It shows that the testing method and the noninvariance degree interpret more variation of Type I error rate than the other factors. However, when detecting truly noninvariant parameters (i.e. intercept or loading), the testing method becomes less critical. Instead, the noninvariance degree, sample size and indicator number interpret more variance of power rates.

Table 3.30   Effect size (η^2) of design factors when varying the indicator number

Design Factor	Type I Error Rate		Power Rate	
	Intercept	Loading	Intercept	Loading
Method	0.148	0.074	0.038	0.005
N	0.020	0.032	0.028	0.123
D	0.065	0.079	0.451	0.281
P	0.007	0.003	0.044	0.087
Method*N	0.011	0.021	0.000	0.000
Method*D	0.041	0.044	0.007	0.003
N*D	0.004	0.016	0.025	0.047
Method*P	0.028	0.030	0.024	0.002
N*P	0.001	0.001	0.000	0.010
D*P	0.005	0.006	0.010	0.037
Method*N*D	0.010	0.011	0.003	0.001
Method*N*P	0.003	0.008	0.002	0.002
Method*D*P	0.012	0.017	0.005	0.001
N*D*P	0.001	0.002	0.003	0.017
Method*N*D*P	0.003	0.004	0.001	0.002

Note: N = sample size; D = degree of noninvariant parameter; P = number of indicators.

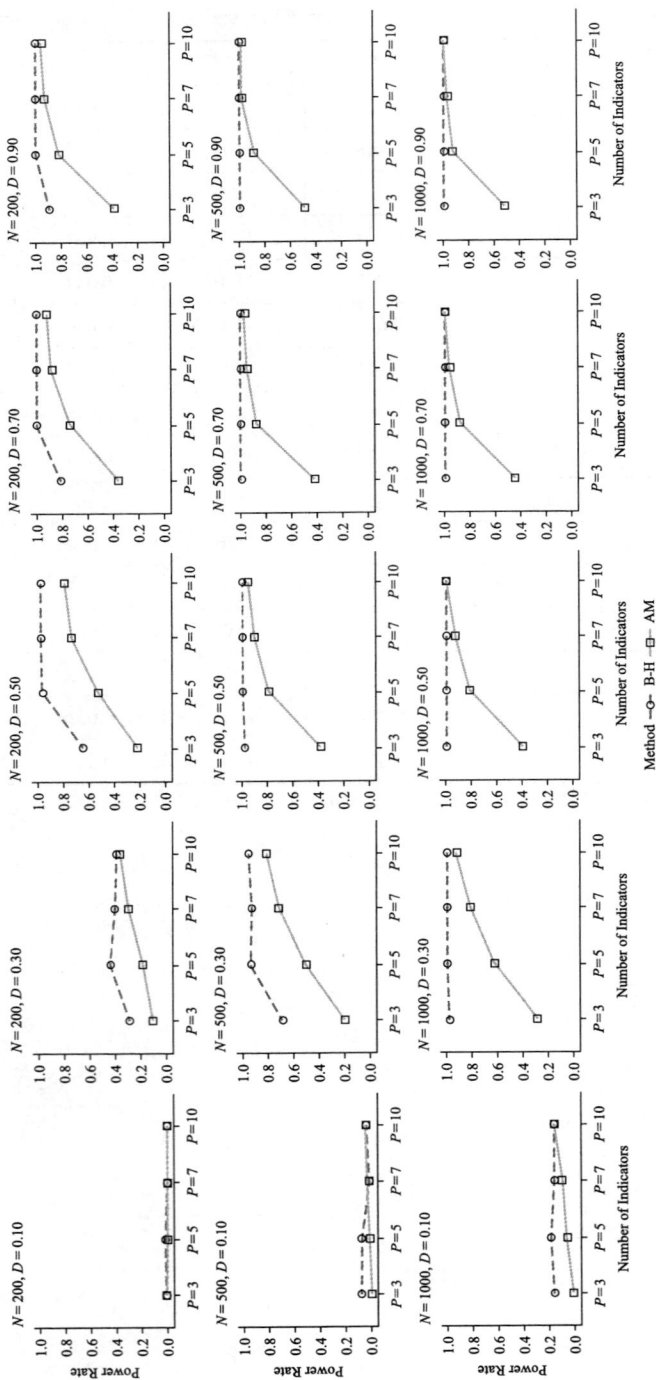

Figure 3.20　Power rates of testing intercepts when varying the indicator number

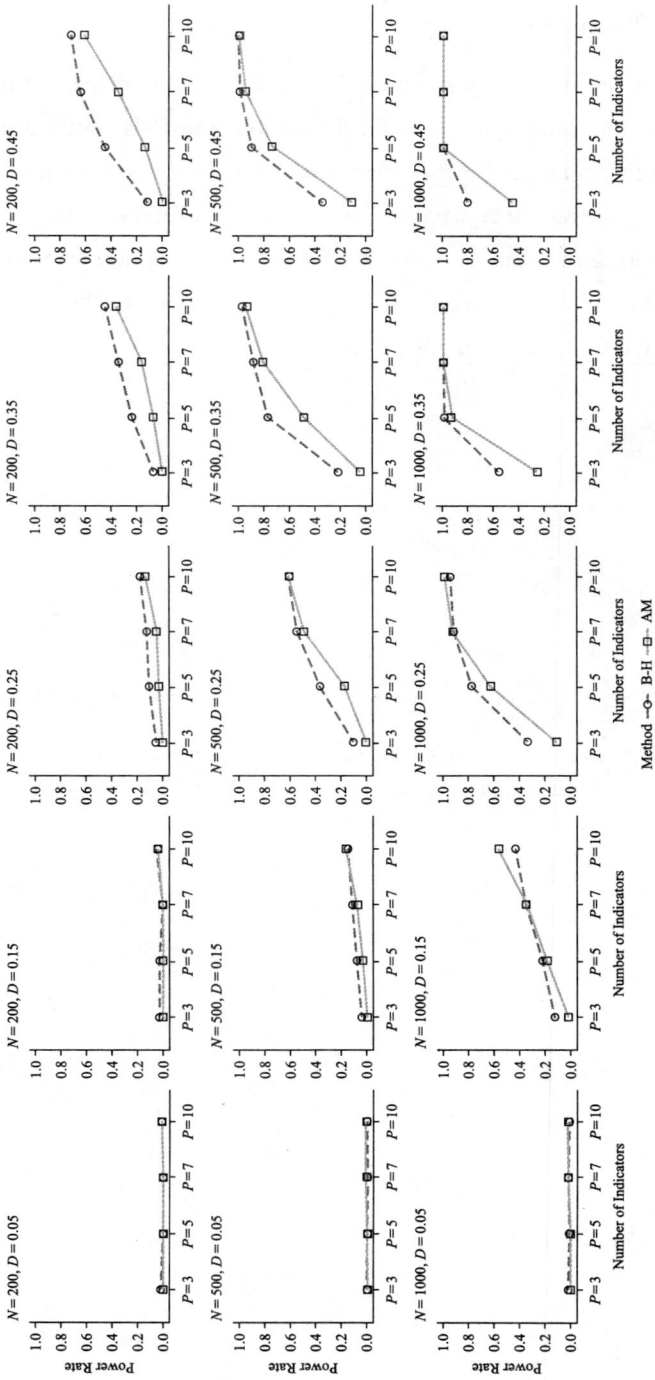

Figure 3.21　Power rates of testing loadings when varying the indicator number

3.7   Chapter Summary

This chapter introduces the research design and results of the simulation study. Three statistical methods, namely the FR method, the B-H method and the AM method are applied to detect measurement models with the violation of MI using a Monte Carlo simulation study design. The processes of generating the simulation data and interpreting the data analysis as well as the evaluation criteria (i.e. Type I error rate and power rate) are described in detail. The results of the simulation study are finally reported for each simulation condition.

Chapter 4 》》

Detection of Measurement Noninvariance in an Empirical Study

4.1 Introduction

In this chapter, the three statistical methods (i.e. the F-R method, the B-H method and the AM method) are applied to detect measurement noninvariance in an empirical dataset (Openness for Problem-Solving Scale in PISA 2012) that is obtained from three countries (China, Australia, and the United States).The performances of the three methods are evaluated according to the invariance/noninvariance patterns identified from the dataset and the results of these applications are reported in detail.

4.2 Empirical Dataset

The empirical dataset is obtained from the Openness for Problem-Solving Scale (OPENPS, coded as ST94) in PISA 2012. The OPENPS is measured by five items (as shown in Table 4.1) in the Student Questionnaire. Each item is on a 5-point Likert scale with five response categories: "Very much like me", "Mostly like me", "Somewhat like me","Not much like me" and "Not at all like me".

Table 4.1　Items of the Openness for Problem-Solving Scale

Items	How well does each of the following statements below describe you?
ST94Q05	I can handle a lot of information.
ST94Q06	I am quick to understand things.
ST94Q09	I seek explanations of things.

(to be continued)

Items	How well does each of the following statements below describe you?
ST94Q10	I can easily link facts together.
ST94Q14	I like to solve complex problems.

In this study, three nationally representative datasets are used: China (CHN, 3429 students), Australia (AUG, 9364 students), and the United States of America (USA, 3145 students). These datasets are selected because of the potential language and cultural differences among these three countries. For example, China is usually considered as a representative country in Eastern culture and America is believed as the representative country in Western culture. Australia belongs to Western culture, which shares similarities with America in both cultural and language aspects. Therefore, it is possible that there exists a contrastive difference in the characteristics of noninvariance between Chinese and American/Australian samples. Since Australia and America share similar language and cultural backgrounds, the characteristics of noninvariance between these two country samples might be similar.

4.3 Data Analysis Procedure

The FR method, the B-H method and the AM method are used for the data calibration among the samples of America, Australia, and China in PISA 2012. The analyses are carried to compare two out of three country samples respectively (i.e. CHN vs. USA, AUS vs. USA, and CHN vs. AUS). The analysis procedures follow those discussed in the section of 3.4. The performances of the three methods are evaluated according to the invariance/noninvariance patterns identified from each of the three pairs.

4.4 The Choice of an RI for the FR Method

An RI has to be selected before conducting the FR analysis. Because the invariance/noninvariance status of the administered five items is unknown, two approaches are applied to select the RI (which was named as FR1 and FR2). In the first approach, the first item (ST94Q05) is chosen as the RI, which is also the default setting of the *Mplus* software. In the second approach, the statistic $Min\chi^2$ developed by Woods (2009) is applied to select the RI. The magnitude of $Min\chi^2$ reflects the degree of difference in item functioning. The smaller the LR statistic, the smaller the item differences between the compared groups. Some researchers approve that this $Min\chi^2$ strategy works well in identifying the invariant indicators (Woods, 2009; Thompson, 2018).

The RI selection based on the $Min\chi^2$ is conducted in the following way. First, a fully constrained baseline model is built after all parameters are constrained to be equal between two country samples. Then, each measurement parameter is freed to construct a series of nested models. The LR test is used to compare each nested model with the fully constrained baseline model. The measurement parameter producing the smallest LR statistic is selected to define the latent scale.

As shown in Table 4.2, the intercept located at ST94Q14 produces the smallest LR statistics when comparing AUS vs. CHN and CHN vs. USA. The intercept located at ST94Q09 produces the smallest LR statistic when comparing AUS vs. USA. The loading located at ST94Q06 produces the smallest LR statistics for all the three between-group comparisons. Therefore, the intercept located at ST94Q14 and the loading located at ST94Q06 are used to define the latent scale when comparing AUS vs. CHN and CHN vs. USA. The intercept located at ST94Q09 and the loading located at ST94Q06 are used to define the latent scale when comparing AUS vs. USA. Based on the results in Table 4.2, the intercept and loading located at the first item (ST94Q05) correspond to large LR statistics, which implies that the first item is more likely to be noninvariant.

Table 4.2　LR statistics of all measurement parameters

Items	AUS vs. CHN	AUS vs. USA	CHN vs. USA
Intercept			
ST94Q05	159.906	9.464	173.743
ST94Q06	12.738	4.939	2.048
ST94Q09	6.088	**1.203**	15.971
ST94Q10	135.621	2.225	112.322
ST94Q14	**4.064**	4.232	**0.088**

(*to be continued*)

Items	AUS vs. CHN	AUS vs. USA	CHN vs. USA
Loading			
ST94Q05	24.022	2.997	1.902
ST94Q06	**0.744**	**0.070**	**0.322**
ST94Q09	117.031	5.953	44.431
ST94Q10	2.535	1.031	2.376
ST94Q14	1.354	3.260	5.527

Notes: USA = the United States of America; AUS = Australia; CHN = China.

4.5　Results of the Empirical Study

The results of identified invariance/noninvariance patterns are presented in Figure 4.1. In this figure, the dark square denotes that the tested parameter is statistically noninvariant between the paired groups. The light gray square denotes that the invariant hypothesis of the tested parameter is not rejected. The middle gray square denotes the corresponding parameter is prefixed as the RI.

When choosing the first item (ST94Q05) as the RI, the invariance/noninvariance patterns estimated by the FR1 method are largely different from those estimated by the B-H method and the AM method. In case of AUS vs. USA, three intercepts (ST94Q06, ST94Q09, and ST94Q10) and one loading (ST94Q09) estimated by the FR1 approach are noninvariant. In contrast, no noninvariant parameter is identified by the B-H method and only one noninvariant loading (ST94Q05) is identified by the AM method. In cases of AUS vs. CHN and CHN vs. USA, the invariance/ noninvariance patterns estimated by the B-H method and the AM method are similar, but different with the pattern estimated by the FR1 method. The difference between the FR1 approach and the other two methods indicates that the former approach is problematic in justifying the noninvariance because the pre-fixed intercept of RI (ST94Q05) might be noninvariant in reality.

If the FR2 approach is chosen instead, all the three methods (FR2, B-H, and AM) produce similar results. In case of AUS vs. USA, the majority of measurement parameters are invariant. Only one intercept (ST94Q05) estimated by the FR2 method and one loading (ST94Q05) estimated by the AM method are noninvariant. In case of AUS vs. CHN, three intercepts (ST94Q05, ST94Q06, and ST94Q09) and one loading (ST94Q09) are discovered to be noninvariant by all the three methods. In case of CHN vs. USA, two intercepts (ST94Q05 and ST94Q10) and one loading (ST94Q09) are discovered to be noninvariant by all the three methods. The similar invariance/noninvariance patterns among the three methods indicate that: 1) The OPENPS measures are more likely invariant between AUS and USA (which were culturally similar) than the other two pairs (which were more culturally distinct); and 2) the FR2 approach works better than the FR1 approach.

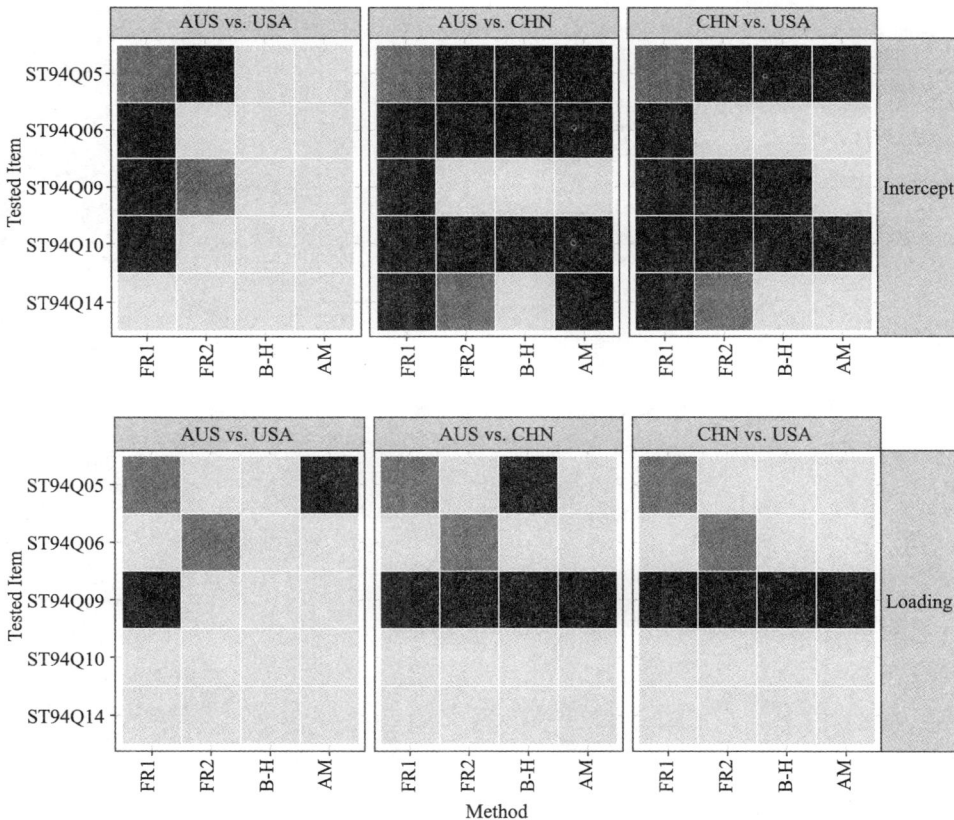

Figure 4.1   Invariance/noninvariance patterns identified for the Openness for
Problem-Solving Scale

4.6 Chapter Summary

In this empirical study, the FR method (FR1 and FR2), the B-H method and the AM method are applied to detect measurement noninvariance in an empirical dataset named Openness for Problem-Solving Scale in PISA 2012 obtained from three countries (China, Australia, and the United States). The invariance/noninvariance patterns identified by both FR1 and FR2 are compared with those identified by the B-H method and the AM method. The results indicate that the FR1 approach is problematic because of incorrectly choosing an item as the RI, no matter which pair of country samples is compared. When the FR2 method is employed, the significance patterns recovered by these three methods are more consistent with each other.

Chapter 5 >>

Conclusions and Recommendations

5.1   Introduction

This chapter first summarizes the findings of the simulation and empirical study about the performances of the three statistical methods in detecting measurement noninvariance, and then discusses the results and implications from the studies. Suggestions on which method is better used for model noninvariance detection is discussed and elaborated. Finally, limitations and future research recommendations are presented.

5.2   Summary of Findings

5.2.1   Simulation Study

The results of the simulation study are summarized separately according to the three different ways used to manipulate the magnitude of model noninvariance.

Magnitude of Model Noninvariance by Varying the Proportion of Noninvariant Indicators

In this section, the noninvariant intercepts/loadings embedded in the models are in different indicators. The model noninvariance is in either one indicator (i.e. low proportion) or two indicators (i.e. high proportion). The other two simulated factors are the sample size and the noninvariance degree. The effect of each simulated factor is interpreted in terms of perfect recovery rate, Type I error rate, and power rate.

No perfect recovery rates are reported for the FR method because the RI is prefixed before any MI testing. For the other two methods (i.e. the B-H method and the AM method), the perfect recovery rates are commonly affected by changing the proportion of noninvariant indicators. When the proportion is low, both methods are possible to achieve high perfect recovery rates. Yet, when the proportion is high, both methods do not perform quite well. Both methods are also impacted by the sample size and noninvariance degree. Comparatively speaking, the B-H method performs better at the medium noninvariance degrees, and the AM method performs better under the conditions of large sample size and large noninvariance degree.

On the Type I error rates, the AM method is the most robust approach among the three methods to resist the Type I errors. The Type I errors are kept at the base level under all simulation conditions. The B-H method follows afterwards and its performance becomes worse as the proportion of noninvariant indicators in the models increases. The existence of noninvariant intercepts/loadings impacts the testing of the other type of parameters. In contrast, when employing the FR method, the noninvariant intercepts/loadings only affects the testing of the same type of parameters. Under such cases, the FR method always leads to more serious Type I errors than the B-H method. In addition, both the FR method and the B-H method are negatively impacted as the sample size, the noninvariance degree and the proportion of noninvariant indicators increase.

As to the power rates, the FR method is unable to detect any noninvariant parameters in the models. In contrast, the B-H method shows the advantages of having the best performance among the three methods. The AM method performs better than the FR method, but worse than the B-H method under most simulation conditions.

Magnitude of Model Noninvariance by Varying the Noninvariance at the Same Indicator

In this section, the high magnitude of model contamination is represented by one indicator which is fully noninvariant at both the intercept and loading. The perfect recovery rates given by the B-H method and the AM method are lowered by the fully noninvariant indicator. The AM method is more severely impacted than the B-H method in general.

The Type I errors given by the AM method are still kept at the base level. The

FR method and the B-H method, however, are affected to a different degree. When choosing the FR method, the addition of noninvariant intercept or loading impacts the testing outcome during testing the same Type of parameters. On the other hand, the added noninvariant loading mitigates the Type I errors for testing intercepts while the added noninvariant intercept has no effect on testing loadings. When choosing the B-H method, the negative impact imposed by adding the noninvariant loading is the largest when the noninvariance degree is medium. The negative impact imposed by adding the noninvariant intercept becomes more severe as the sample size and the noninvariance degree increase.

The power rates given by the B-H method and the AM method are impacted differently according to the type of added noninvariant parameters. If the noninvariant loading is added, the B-H method is not affected while the AM method reports lower power rates. In contrast, if the noninvariant intercept is added, the AM method is not impacted while the B-H method reports higher power rates.

Magnitude of Model Noninvariance by the Variation of the Indicator Numbers

In this section, the magnitude of model noninvariance is manipulated by varying the indicator numbers in the models. The larger the indicator number, the less magnitude the model noninvariance.

When the AM method is applied, the perfect recovery rates increase with the increase of the indicator number. For the B-H method, the effect of indicator number is different according to the location of the noninvariant parameter. If the noninvariance is located at the loading, the perfect recovery rates increase when administrating a large number of indicators. But if the noninvariance is located at the intercept, the perfect recovery rates increase only at the medium noninvariance degree.

For the effect of indicator number on the Type I error rate, changing the indicator number do not affect the AM method but affect the other two methods. When the B-H method is applied, the increase of indicator number reduces the occurrence of Type I errors in general. However, when choosing the FR method, the increase of indicator number can enlarge the Type I errors under some conditions.

During testing the truly noninvariant parameters, the power rates estimated by the B-H method and the AM method become larger with the increase of indicator numbers. This effect is especially apparent when the noninvariance degree is high.

5.2.2 Empirical Study

During the empirical data analysis, the FR method is conducted by using two strategies to select the RI (FR1 and FR2). FR1 chooses the first item (ST94Q05) as the RI and FR2 chooses the parameters of RI based on the statistic $Min\chi^2$. The invariance/noninvariance patterns identified by both FR approaches are compared with those identified by the B-H method and the AM method.

The invariance/noninvariance patterns recovered by the FR1 method are largely different from the other two methods, no matter which pair of country samples is compared. In contrast, when the FR2 method is employed, the significance patterns recovered by these three methods are more consistent with each other. In case of AUS vs. USA, it is found that the majority of measurement parameters can be invariant. In cases of AUS vs. CHN and CHN vs. USA, the noninvariant parameters identified by these three methods are similar. These findings suggest that the FR1 approach is problematic because of incorrectly choosing the first item (ST94Q05) as the RI.

5.3 Comments on the Performances of the Three Methods

This study aims to investigate the differences among the three methods to correctly identify the true measurement models which are contaminated by noninvariance. Overall, the FR method, for which the RI is prefixed as noninvariant, performs worse than the other two methods. The B-H method shows the advantages of having higher powers to detect noninvariant parameters. Comparatively, the AM method shows the advantages of controlling the Type I errors.

The popularity of the FR method in MI testing has many reasons. But two of them are fundamental. First, it is believed that the FR method can perform well to precisely identify the invariant and noninvariant model components if the RI is selected correctly. Second, the RI can be decided correctly based on statistical evidence. Hence, the performance of the FR method ultimately depends on to what extent the RI will meet these requirements.

To check the first belief, besides the results reported in Chapter 3 where the RI for the FR method is truly noninvariant, the FR method is also conducted by choosing one truly invariant indicator as the RI. The results confirm that the FR method performs well in controlling the Type I errors. No matter whether the intercepts or loadings are tested, the Type I error rates are as low as the base level. The FR method can retrieve high power rates in detecting noninvariance when the sample size and the noninvariance degree are large enough. These results are consistent with the findings in some previous studies (e.g. Meade & Lautenschlager, 2004; Jung & Yoon, 2016). The values of the FR method with correct RI setting come from the features of its FR model. Since all the tested parameters are freely estimated, the FR model avoids the incorrect equality constraints for those truly noninvariant parameters.

On the second belief, many researchers attempt to find a robust statistical approach to identify one appropriate RI. These statistical approaches are developed from different perspectives. For example, the RI is selected as the indicator that has the largest factor loading (*MaxL*; see Stark et al., 2006), the indicator that has the smallest LR statistic (*Minχ^2*; see Woods, 2009), or the indicator that produces the smallest standardized parameter difference (Bayesian selection index; see Shi et al., 2017). These statistics provide information on which indicator is more likely to be invariant than the other indicators, but they are unable to determine whether the selected RI is truly invariant or not. Hence, the reliance on statistical evidence for the choice of an RI is left with doubt if no additional empirical evidence is discovered to support it. The uncertainty of RI choice endangers the recovery of true measurement models.

The research results on the FR method in the simulation study are consistent with the critiques from previous studies (e.g. Raykov et al., 2012; Yoon & Millsap, 2007; Johnson et al., 2009; Lopez Rivas et al., 2009). The FR method performs worse in the following aspects if the RI is not truly invariant. First, no models can be perfectly recovered by this method for all measurement parameters. Second, the Type I errors are always larger than those obtained from the B-H method and the AM method. The Type I errors consistently increase as the sample size, the noninvariance degree, and the magnitude of noninvariance increase. Third, the power rates of detecting the noninvariance are reduced to very low values under all the simulation conditions.

Unlike the FR method, as an alternative MGCFA approach without the requirement of RI setting, the B-H method circumvents the problems caused by the risk of an inappropriate RI (Raykov et al., 2013). The advantages of the B-H method come from its initial aim to increase the power rates. It is designed as a weak form of family wise error rate controlling procedure (i.e. FDR controlling procedure; Benjamini & Hochberg, 1995). By applying this FDR controlling procedure, the high power rates are warranted, and at the same time, the Type I errors are controlled at a certain level.

The results in the simulation study prove that the B-H method performs the best to obtain higher power rates than the other two methods. As mentioned before, the FR method shows no powers to correctly identify the model noninvariance. Although the AM method is also able to recover the model noninvariance to some extent, this method do not perform as well as the B-H method. In general, the B-H method has more powers than the AM method during the detection of model noninvariance. Moreover, compared to the AM method, the power rates estimated by the B-H method are more positively enhanced by increasing the sample size and noninvariance degree, and are less negatively compromised by enlarging the magnitude of model noninvariance.

On the other hand, the baseline model applied in the B-H method needs to be fully constrained (Williams et al., 1999; Raykov et al., 2013). Forcing all the indicators to be group equivalent in the baseline model can be problematic for the accuracy of LR tests if some parameters in the models are actually noninvariant (Stark et al., 2006; Kim & Yoon, 2011). In particular, if models are contaminated by noninvariance to a large extent, the Type I errors can be impacted in the following two aspects.

First, the Type I errors can increase as the model contamination becomes severe and the sample size becomes large (Kim & Yoon, 2011). A larger extent of model contamination indicates that the assumption for the full invariance baseline model is more severely violated. A larger sample size implies that LR statistic will be more sensitive in MI testing. The findings in this study conform to these two arguments.

When increasing the noninvariance degree or the magnitude of model noninvariance embedded in the models, large Type I errors emerge. Likewise, larger sample sizes always cause more severe Type I errors.

Second, the accuracy of detecting one type of invariant parameter may be compromised due to the existence of the other noninvariant parameter in the models. As found in this study, using the B-H method, the existence of noninvariant loadings causes more Type I errors while testing the intercepts, and the existence of noninvariant intercepts causes more Type I errors while testing the loadings. In contrast, when applying the FR method, which is based on the free baseline approach, the existence of noninvariant loadings only slightly compromises the detection of intercepts, and the existence of noninvariant intercepts do not impact the detection of loadings.

Unlike previous two methods, the fundamental assumption of the AM method is that a pattern of approximate MI holds in the data. It implicates that if this fundamental assumption is not violated (i.e. the percentage of model noninvariance < 25%), the AM method is able to perform well at the model level. In other words, the true measurement model which is partially noninvariant will be recovered well and the perfect recovery rates will be high.

This study finds that even though the generated datasets are below the recommended percentage of model noninvariance, the perfect recovery rates are not high under all simulation conditions. The perfect recovery rates are low while increasing the magnitude of model noninvariance, decreasing the sample size and the noninvariance degree.

The reason for the low perfect recovery rates is mainly due to the low power rates during detecting the truly noninvariant parameters in the models. The Type I errors estimated by the AM method are always as low as the basis level, and therefore, have no large impact on the perfect recovery rate. However, the power rates are reduced by increasing the magnitude of model noninvariance (i.e. adding extra noninvariant parameters or reducing the indicator number). In addition, the power rate is small if the sample size and the noninvariance degree are not large enough.

These results have two implications about the AM method. First, this method is able to control the Type I errors if its fundamental assumption of approximate MI is not violated. Second, the conditions leading to low power rates are also the conditions compromising the recovery of true measurement models.

5.4　Implications and Recommendations

As stated by Kwok et al. (2018: 2), "Measurement models are an important part of SEM, and the flexibility of SEM not only allows researchers to develop and validate new scales but also provides a simple and feasible platform for examining the potential differences between groups and populations through the test of MI."

All three methods studied in this thesis fall within the framework of SEM, but address the MI testing problem from different perspectives. Which method is a better choice depends on the extent its basic assumption is satisfied and how effective it is in correctly recovering the true model parameters.

The major concern for the FR method is the appropriateness of the selected RI. As discussed previously, the choice of an RI cannot completely rely on statistical evidence unless it can also be well supported by theoretical or empirical evidence. Different statistical approaches may give ambiguous suggestions for the RI choice during empirical data analysis. The wrong choice of an RI endangers the interpretation of the outcome reported by the FR method, as demonstrated in this research. The FR method may not be safely applied unless the uncertainty related to the RI is well solved.

The B-H method is conducted based on the fully constrained baseline model, which indicates that this method might be compromised if models are contaminated by a large magnitude of noninvariance. However, with the application of the FDR controlling procedure, the B-H method can still provide higher powers than the other two methods, even though the magnitude of noninvariance is large. Compared to the other two methods, the B-H method is more powerful to screen out the noninvariant components.

The optimization of parameter estimates based on the plausibility of configural invariance makes the AM method a good exploratory procedure in MI testing. However, the application of optimization procedure also indicates that the parameters are only approximately estimated and the estimates may not conform to the true values precisely. To what extent the true measurement model is recovered depends on whether the optimization of the loss function works properly or not. If the models are not highly contaminated and the approximate MI is plausible in the dataset, the AM method could be applied to lower the risks of false positive findings. Hence, this method is more conservative than the other two methods in identifying the model noninvariance. Because it is usually unclear to what extent the real data will meet the assumption of approximate MI, the outcome for the invariance/noninvariance of measurement parameters should be interpreted with caution.

5.5 Limitations

The present research has limitations that need to be mentioned. First, this study assumed the noninvariant parameters always take higher values in the focal group than the reference group, so that the direction of model noninvariance is uniform. The effect of noninvariance direction on the performance of the three methods was not studied. It is recommended that future studies incorporate different directions of noninvariance in the models, and examine the three methods' performance under such conditions. Second, the indicators were assumed to be continuous and normally distributed. It is not uncommon that the measures in surveys or questionnaires may have fewer than 5-7 categories. In such circumstances, the assumption of approximate normality is severely violated. In future studies, indicators can be simulated as categorical ones. Third, the present study only considers the parameter noninvariance between two groups. The magnitude of noninvariance may also vary at the group level where either a few or a large number of groups are contaminated by noninvariant parameters. Future studies might consider simulating the variation of noninvariance in multiple groups. Finally, beyond the three methods studied in this research, there are also other statistical methods (e.g. Exploratory Structural Equation Modeling, Asparouhov & Muthén, 2009; Bayesian Structural Equation Modeling, Muthén & Asparouhov, 2012) within the SEM framework that can be used to explore the invariant/noninvariant status of measurement parameters. Future studies may be conducted by including these methods to detect the violation of MI.

Appendix A
Technical Details for the B-H Method

1. The Concept of FDR

To interpret the concept of FDR, suppose there is a multiple testing scenario where m null hypotheses are to be tested simultaneously. Part of these null hypotheses are true (denoted as m_0), and the others are not true (denoted as m_1). After the significance testing, these null hypotheses fall into four categories. The numbers of all possible testing outcomes can be organized in Table A.1.

Table A.1　The number of discovery/nondiscovery after m null hypotheses

	H_0 retained	H_0 rejected	Total
H_0 True	True Nondiscovery *(TN)*	False Discovery *(FD)*	m_0
H_0 False	False Nondiscovery *(FN)*	True Discovery *(TD)*	m_1
Total	Nondiscovery *(N)*	Discovery *(D)*	m

When multiple null hypotheses are tested simultaneously, the Type I error can be either uncorrected or family-wise adjusted. Based on the notation in Table A.1, the uncorrected error rate, also named per-comparison Type I error rate (PCER), is controlled as:

$$P\{FD_i > 0\} \leqslant \alpha \quad (1 \leqslant i \leqslant m),$$

where α is the preset Type I error rate (e.g. $\alpha = 0.05$).

When the number of tested null hypotheses is large, the Type I error for the whole set of testing is large. In other words, more numbers of true null hypotheses will be falsely rejected. Then, the family-wise error rate (FWER) is useful to control the overall Type I error. The controlled error rate is:

$$P\{FD > 0\} \leqslant \alpha$$

For example, if Bonferroni's adjusting approach is adopted, the Type I error for the single null hypothesis is largely reduced. Per-comparison Type I error rate will be controlled as:

$$P\{FD_i > 0\} \leqslant \alpha/m \quad (1 \leqslant i \leqslant m)$$

However, in some cases, the FWER controlling methods are too conservative and not practically meaningful. For instance, with large number of null hypotheses to be tested, the power of True Discovery will be too low. To alleviate the low power of traditional FWER methods, FDR is perceived as a new way to control FWER for the purpose of achieving more power. Following the notation in Table A.1, FDR is controlled as:

$$FDR = E\left(\frac{FD}{D}\right) \leqslant \alpha$$

Hence, it can be seen that *FDR* is conceptualized as the ratio between the number of falsely rejected null hypothesis (*FD*) and the total number of rejected null hypothesis ($D = FD + TD$; including both correctly and falsely rejected null hypotheses). For the situation when there is no rejected null hypothesis (that is, $D = 0$), *FDR* is defined as zero.

2. Steps of the B-H Procedure in Testing Parameter Noninvariance

When there are k indicators, an overall series of $2k$ hypothesis testing are furnished for k loadings and k intercepts. With all p values obtained from $2k$ individual parameter testing, the B-H method is used to determine which tested parameters are noninvariant.

Let $P_{(i)}$ ($i = 1, \ldots, 2k$) be the p values of the $2k$ hypotheses under consideration. The steps for employing the B-H method are:

(1) Rank $P_{(i)}$ sequentially from small to large values. That is, let $P_{(1)} < \ldots < P_{(2k)}$ denote the ordered p values;

(2) Given a significance level α (e.g. $\alpha = 0.05$), define a set of ratios for $2k$ null hypothesis testing as:

$$l_i = i\alpha/C_{2k} \, 2k \text{ and } R = max\{i: P_{(i)} < i\},$$

where $C_{2k} = \sum_{i=1}^{2k} (1/i)$ when p values are dependent (Benjamini & Yekutieli, 2001).

(3) Let $T = P_{(R)}$, T is the B-H rejection threshold;

(4) Reject all null hypotheses when $P_i \leqslant T$.

Appendix B

Technical Details for the AM Method

1. The Rationale of the AM Method

In Asparouhov & Muthén's (2014) seminal article, the optimization process was mathematically illustrated. In the root configural model, suppose the loading and intercept parameter estimates for the kth indicator in group g are denoted as $v_{kg,root}$ and $\lambda_{kg,\,root}$, respectively. Then, when freeing the fixed factor means and variances in the root configural model to establish a re-specified model, a new set of loading and intercept estimates can be obtained (denoted as $v_{kg,1}$ and $\lambda_{kg,1}$, respectively). These two models will share the same likelihood, but the model parameter estimates are different.

The two sets of indicator parameter estimates are related. Specifically, the new estimates in the respecified model can be transformed according to the known estimates from the root configural model and the factor means and variances in the new model, which are shown in the following equations.

$$\lambda_{kg,1} = \frac{\lambda_{kg,root}}{\sqrt{\phi_g^*}},$$

$$v_{kg,1} = v_{kg,root} - \kappa_g^* \frac{\lambda_{kg,root}}{\sqrt{\phi_g^*}},$$

where κ_g^* and ϕ_g^* represent the latent factor mean and variance in group g.

With one set of arbitrary choice of κ_g^* and ϕ_g^*, one new set of indicator parameters $(v_{kg,1}, \lambda_{kg,1})$ for the kth indicator in group g can be determined. We hope to choose the values of κ_g^* and ϕ_g^* so that the amount of MI is maximized. To minimize the total amount of measurement noninvariance, a loss/simplicity function that accumulates the total noninvariance can be defined as:

$$F = \sum_k \sum_{g1<g2} w_{g1,g2} f(\lambda_{kg1,1} - \lambda_{kg2,1}) + \sum_k \sum_{g1<g2} w_{g1,g2} f(v_{kg1,1} - v_{kg2,1}),$$

where $w_{g1,g2} = \sqrt{N_{g1}N_{g2}}$ represents the weight, and f represents a component loss function (CLF) (Jennrich, 2006), which is defined as:

$$f(x) = \sqrt{\sqrt{x^2 + \varepsilon}}$$

In the alignment optimization procedure, ε is a small number ($\varepsilon = 0.01$). A positive ε is used so that the CLF has a continuous first derivative, simplifying optimization of the total loss function,

The CLF simplicity function helps the respecified model become identified. The total loss will be minimized at a solution where there are a few large noninvariant measurement parameters and many approximately invariant parameters (Asparouhov & Muthén, 2014).

2. Used Criteria in Justifying Parameter Noninvariance

The information to evaluate the degree of measurement parameter noninvariance can be obtained from three resources (Asparouhov & Muthén, 2014).

First, the invariance hypothesis for one measurement parameter is conducted through a pairwise comparison test across groups. If the p value is bigger than a preselected α level (such as 0.01, recommended by Asparouhov & Muthén, 2014), the equality hypothesis is rejected. The tested parameter is labeled as noninvariant between the involved groups.

Second, the degree of noninvariance can be evaluated based on the contribution of each parameter to the optimized simplicity function. The contribution reflects the level of noninvariance for the parameter. The smaller the contribution is, the more invariant the parameter will be.

Third, the evaluation of noninvariance can refer to the effect size measure R^2. The R^2 measure describes the variability explained in the measurement parameters across groups that is due to group mean and variance differences (Asparouhov & Muthén, 2014; Flake & McCoach, 2018). For intercepts and loadings, the formulas are:

$$R^2_{int} = 1 - V(v_0 - v - \kappa_g \lambda)/V(v_0)$$
$$R^2_{load} = 1 - V(\lambda_0 - \sqrt{\psi_g}\lambda)/V(\lambda_0),$$

where v is the average aligned intercept and λ is the average aligned loading across groups. The R^2 measure is a useful descriptive statistic for the degree of noninvariance which can be absorbed by group varying factor means and variances. A high R^2 value indicates a high degree of parameter invariance and vise versa.

References

Asparouhov, T., & Muthén, B. Exploratory structural equation modeling[J]. *Structural Equation Modeling*, 2009, *16*(3): 397-438.

Asparouhov, T., & Muthén, B. Multiple-group factor analysis alignment[J]. *Structural Equation Modeling*, 2014, *21*(4): 495-508.

Barendse, M. T., Oort, F. J., & Garst, G. J. A. Using restricted factor analysis with latent moderated structures to detect uniform and nonuniform measurement bias: A simulation study[J]. *Advances in Statistical Analysis*, 2010, *94*(2): 117-127.

Benjamini, Y., & Hochberg, Y. Controlling the false discovery rate: A practical and powerful approach to multiple testing[J]. *Journal of the Royal Statistical Society, Series B(Methodological)*, 1995, *57*(1): 289-300.

Benjamini, Y., & Yekutieli, D. The control of the false discovery rate in multiple testing under dependency[J]. *The Annals of Statistics*, 2001, *29*(4): 1165-1188.

Bollen, K. A. *Structural Equations with Latent Variables*[M]. London: John Wiley & Sons, 1989.

Brannick, M. T. Critical comments on applying covariance structure modeling[J]. *Journal of Organizational Behavior*, 1995, *16*(3): 201-213.

Buss, A. R., & Royce, J. R. Detecting cross-cultural commonalties and differences: Intergroup factor analysis[J]. *Psychological Bulletin*, 1975, *82*(1): 128-136.

Byrne, B. M., Shavelson, R. J., & Muthén, B. Testing for the equivalence of factor covariance and mean structures: The issue of partial measurement invariance[J]. *Psychological Bulletin*, 1989, *105*(3): 456-466.

Byrne, B. M., & van de Vijve, F. J. The maximum likelihood alignment approach to testing for approximate measurement invariance: A paradigmatic cross-cultural application[J]. *Psicothema*, 2017, *29*(4): 535-551.

Cheung, G. W., & Lau, R. S. A direct comparison approach for testing measurement invariance[J]. *Organizational Research Methods*, 2012, *15*(2): 167-198.

Cheung, G. W., & Rensvold, R. B. Cross-cultural comparisons using non-invariant measurement items[J]. *Applied Behavioral Science Review*, 1998, *6*(1): 93-110.

Cheung, G. W., & Rensvold, R. B. Testing factorial invariance across groups: A reconceptualization and proposed new method[J]. *Journal of Management*, 1999, *25*(1): 1-27.

Cheung, G. W., & Rensvold, R. B. Evaluating goodness-of-fit indexes for testing measurement invariance[J]. *Structural Equation Modeling*, 2002, *9*(2):233-255.

Davidov, E., Dülmer, H., Schlüter, E., Schmidt, P., & Meuleman, B. Using a multilevel structural equation modeling approach to explain cross-cultural measurement noninvariance[J]. *Journal of Cross-Cultural Psychology*, 2012, *43*(4): 558-575.

Davidov, E., Meuleman, B., Cieciuch, J., Schmidt, P., & Billiet, J. Measurement equivalence in cross-national research[J]. *Annual Review of Sociology*, 2014(40): 55-75.

Dimitrov, D. M. Testing for factorial invariance in the context of construct validation[J]. *Measurement and Evaluation in Counseling and Development*, 2010, *43*(2): 121-149.

DiStefano, C. The impact of categorization with confirmatory factor analysis[J]. *Structural Equation Modeling*, 2002, *9*(3): 327-346.

Flake, J. K., & McCoach, D. B. An investigation of the alignment method with polytomous indicators under conditions of partial measurement invariance[J]. *Structural Equation Modeling*, 2018, *25*(1): 56-70.

Flowers, C. P., Raju, N. S., & Oshima, T. C. A comparison of measurement equivalence methods based on confirmatory factor analysis and item response Theory[A]. New Orleans: Annual Meeting of the National Council on Measurement in Education (NCME), 2002.

Finch, W. H., & French, B. F. Using exploratory factor analysis for locating invariant referents in factor invariance studies[J]. *Journal of Modern Applied Statistical Methods*, 2008a, *7*(1): 223-233.

Finch, W. H., & French, B. F. Comparing factor loadings in exploratory factor analysis: A new randomization test[J]. *Journal of Modern Applied Statistical*

Methods, 2008b, *7*(2): 376-384.

French, B. G., & Finch, W. H. Multigroup confirmatory factor analysis: Locating the invariant referent sets[J]. *Structural Equation Modeling*, 2008, *15*(1): 96-113.

Herzog, W., Boomsma. A., & Reinecke, S. The model-size effect on traditional and modified tests of covariance structures[J]. *Structural Equation Modeling*, 2007, *14*(3): 361-390.

Horn, J. L., McArdle, J. J., & Mason, R. When is invariance not invariant: A practical scientist's look at the ethereal concept of factor invariance[J]. *Southern Psychologist*, 1983, *1*(4): 179-188.

Horn, J. L., & McArdle, J. J. A practical and theoretical guide to measurement invariance in aging research[J]. *Experimental Aging Research*, 1992, *18*(3): 117-144.

Jang, S., Kim, E. S., Cao, C., Allen, T. D., Cooper, C. L., Lapierre, L. M., & Abarca, N. Measurement invariance of the satisfaction with life scale across 26 countries[J]. *Journal of Cross-Cultural Psychology*, 2017, *48*(4): 560-576.

Jennrich, R. I. Rotation to simple loadings using component loss functions: The oblique case[J]. *Psychometrika*, 2006, *71*(1): 173-191.

Jöreskog, K. G. Simultaneous factor analysis in several populations[J]. *Psychometrika*, 1971, *36*(4): 409-426.

Johnson, E. C., Meade, A. W., & DuVernet, A. M. The role of referent indicators in tests of measurement invariance[J]. *Structural Equation Modeling*, 2009, *16*(4): 642-657.

Jung, E., & Yoon, M. Comparisons of three empirical methods for partial factorial invariance: Forward, backward, and factor-ratio tests[J]. *Structural Equation Modeling*, 2016, *23*(4):567-584.

Kelloway, E. K. Structural equation modeling in perspective[J]. *Journal of Organizational Behavior*, 1995, *16*(3): 215-224.

Kwok, O. M., Cheung, M. W., Jak, S., Ryu, E., & Wu, J. Y. Editorial: Recent advancements in Structural Equation Modeling (SEM): From both methodological and application perspectives[J]. *Frontiers in Psychology*, 2018(9):1936.

Kim, E. S. and Yoon, M. Testing measurement invariance: A comparison of multiple-group categorical CFA and IRT[J]. *Structural Equation Modeling*, 2011, *18*(2): 212-228.

Little, T. D. Mean and covariance structures (MACS) analyses of cross-cultural data: Practical and theoretical issues[J]. *Multivariate Behavioral Research*, 1997, *32*(1): 53-76.

Little, T. D., Slegers, D. W., & Card, N. A. A Non-arbitrary method of identifying and scaling latent variables in SEM and MACS models[J]. *Structural Equation Modeling*, 2006, *13*(1): 59-72.

Lomazzi, V. Using alignment optimization to test the measurement invariance of gender role attitudes in 59 countries[J]. *Methods, Data, Analyses*, 2018, *12*(1): 77-103.

Lopez Rivas, G. E., Stark, S., & Chernyshenko, O. S. The effects of referent item parameters on differential item functioning detection using the free baseline likelihood ratio test[J]. *Applied Psychological Measurement*, 2009, *33*(4): 251-265.

Marsh, H. W., & Hocevar, D. Application of confirmatory factor analysis to the study of self-concept: First- and higher order factor models and their invariance across groups[J]. *Psychological Bulletin*, 1985, *97*(3): 562-582.

Meade, A. W., & Lautenschlager, G. J. A comparison of item response theory and confirmatory factor analytic methodologies for establishing measurement equivalence/invariance[J]. *Organizational Research Methods*, 2004, *7*(4): 361-388.

Meade, A. W., & Wright, N. A. Solving the measurement invariance anchor item problem in item response theory[J]. *Journal of Applied Psychology*, 2012, *97*(5): 1016-1031.

Mellenbergh, G. J. Item bias and item response theory[J]. *International Journal of Educational Research*, 1989, *13*(2): 127-143.

Meredith, W. Measurement invariance, factor analysis and factorial invariance[J]. *Psychometrika*, 1993, *58*(4): 525-543.

Millsap, R. E. *Statistical Approaches to Measurement Invariance*[M]. New York: Routledge, 2011.

Millsap, R. E., & Meredith, W. Factorial invariance: Historical perspectives and new problems[M]// R. Cudeck & R. C. MacCallum. *Factor Analysis at 100: Historical Developments and Future Directions*. Hillsdale: Lawrence Erlbaum Associates Publishers, 2007: 131-152.

Millsap, R. E., & Yun-Tein, J. Assessing factorial invariance in ordered categorical measures[J]. *Multivariate Behavioral Research*, 2004, *39*(3): 479-515.

Moshagen, M. The model size effect in SEM: Inflated goodness-off it statistics are due to the size of the covariance matrix[J]. *Structural Equation Modeling*, 2012, *19*(1): 86-98.

Mullen, M. Diagnosing measurement equivalence in cross-national research[J]. *Journal of International Business Studies*, 1995, *26*(3): 573-596.

Munck, I., Barber, C., & Torney-Purta, J. Measurement invariance in comparing attitudes toward immigrants among youth across Europe in 1999 and 2009: The alignment method applied to IEA CIVED and ICCS[J]. *Sociological Methods & Research*, 2018, *47*(4): 687-728.

Muthén, B., & Asparouhov, T. Bayesian Structural Equation Modeling: A more flexible representation of substantive theory[J]. *Psychological Methods*, 2012, *17*(3): 313-335.

Muthén, B., & Asparouhov, T. IRT studies of many groups: The alignment method[J]. *Frontiers in Psychology*, 2014(5): 978.

Muthén, B., & Asparouhov, T. Recent methods for the study of measurement invariance with many groups: alignment and random effects[J]. *Sociological Methods & Research*, 2018, *47*(4): 637-664.

Nye, C., Bradburn, J., Olenick, J., Bialko, C., & Drasgow F. How big are my effects? Examining the magnitude of effect sizes in studies of measurement equivalence[J]. *Organizational Research Methods*, 2019, *22*(3): 678-709.

Oberski, D. L. Evaluating sensitivity of parameters of interest to measurement invariance in latent variable models[J]. *Political Analysis*, 2014, *22*(1): 45-60.

Raykov, T., Dimitrov, D. M., Marcoulides, G. A., Li, T., & Menold, N. Examining measurement invariance and differential item functioning with discrete latent construct indicators: A note on a multiple testing procedure[J]. *Educational and*

Psychological Measurement, 2018, *78*(2): 343-352.

Raykov, T., Marcoulides, G. A., Harrison, M., & Zhang, M. On the dependability of a popular procedure for studying measurement invariance: A cause for concern?[J]. *Structural Equation Modeling*, 2020, *27*(4): 649-656.

Raykov, T., Marcoulides, G. A., & Li, C.-H. Measurement invariance for latent constructs in multiple populations: A critical view and refocus[J]. *Educational and Psychological Measurement*, 2012, *72*(6):954-974.

Raykov, T., Marcoulides, G. A., & Millsap, R. E. Factorial invariance in multiple populations: A multiple testing procedure[J]. *Educational and Psychological Measurement*, 2013, *73*(4): 713-727.

Reise, S. P., Widaman, K. F., & Pugh, R. H. Confirmatory Factor-Analysis and Item Response Theory: Two approaches for exploring measurement invariance[J]. *Psychological Bulletin*, 1993, *114*(3): 552-566.

Schmitt, N., & Kuljanin, G. Measurement invariance: Review of practice and implications[J]. *Human Resource Management Review*, 2008, *18*(4): 210-222.

Shi, D., Lee, T., & Terry, R. A. Revisiting the model size effect in Structural Equation Modeling[J]. *Structural Equation Modeling*, 2018, *25*(1): 21-40.

Shi, D., Song, H., Liao, X., Terry, R., & Snyder, L. A. Bayesian SEM for specification search problems in testing factorial invariance[J]. *Multivariate Behavioral Research*, 2017, *52*(4): 430-444.

Singh, J. Measurement issues in cross-national research[J]. *Journal of International Business Studies*, 1995, *26*(3): 597-619.

Stark, S., Chernyshenko, O. S., & Drasgow, F. Detecting differential item functioning with confirmatory factor analysis and item response theory: Toward a unified strategy[J]. *Journal of Applied Psychology*, 2006, *91(6)*: 1292-1306.

Steenkamp, J. E. M., & Baumgartner, H. Assessing measurement invariance in cross-national consumer research[J]. *Journal of Consumer Research*, 1998, *25*(1): 78-90.

Steinberg, L. The consequences of pairing questions: Context effects in personality measurement[J]. *Journal of Personality and Social Psychology*, 2001, *81*(2): 332-342.

Suzuki, S., & Rancer, A. S. Argumentativeness and verbal aggressiveness: Testing for conceptual and measurement equivalence across cultures[J]. *Communication Monographs*, 1994, *61*(3): 256-279.

Vandenberg, R. J., & Lance, C. E. A review and synthesis of the measurement invariance literature: Suggestions, practices, and recommendations for organizational research[J]. *Organizational Research Methods*, 2000, *3*(1): 4-70.

Whittaker, T. A. Using the modification index and standardized expected parameter change for model modification[J]. *The Journal of Experimental Education*, 2012, *80*(1): 26-44.

Widaman, K. F., & Reise, S. P. Exploring the measurement invariance of psychological instruments: Applications in the substance use domain[M]// K. J. Bryant, M. Windle, & S. G. West. *The Science of Prevention: Methodological Advances from Alcohol and Substance Abuse Research*. Washington: American Psychological Association, 1997: 281-324.

Williams, V. S., Jones, L. V., & Tukey, J. W. Controlling error in multiple comparisons, with examples from state-to-state differences in educational achievement[J]. *Journal of Educational and Behavioral Statistics*, 1999, *24*(1): 42-69.

Woods, C. M. Empirical selection of anchors for tests of differential item functioning[J]. *Applied Psychological Measurement*, 2009, *33*(1): 42-57.

Yoon, M., & Millsap, R. E. Detecting violations of factorial invariance using data-based specification searches: A Monte Carlo study[J]. *Structural Equation Modeling*, 2007, *14*(3): 435-463.

Yuan, K. H., Tian, Y., & Yanagihara, H. Empirical correction to the likelihood ratio statistic for structural equation modeling with many variables[J]. *Psychometrika*, 2015, *80*(2): 379-405.

Postscript

At the time when this book is taking its shape, I am full of gratitude to all those people who have helped me in the process to make this book come into existence.

I would like to express my deepest gratitude to my academic advisor, Dr. Tenko Raykov, who guided me with his expertise through my research. Dr. Raykov initiated my interest in the topic, encouraged me and supported me throughout the writing of the whole book. I would also like to express my sincere appreciation to Dr. Mark D. Reckase, Dr. Richard Houang, and Dr. Ryan Bowles, for their valuable and inspiring suggestions, the patience and time that are devoted to my study.

My hearty thanks also go to Qilu Normal University, which offers me financial support and helps put this book finally to press.

Last but not the least, I would like to express my heartfelt thanks to my parents, my wife and my children for their unconditional love and endless support to me in the process of my study, without which I would not have accomplished so far.

张明才

September, 2022